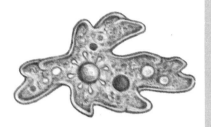

LIFE ON EARTH
Biology Today

The RANDOM HOUSE
LIBRARY OF KNOWLEDGE™

seed

stalk

leaf

prop roots

soil

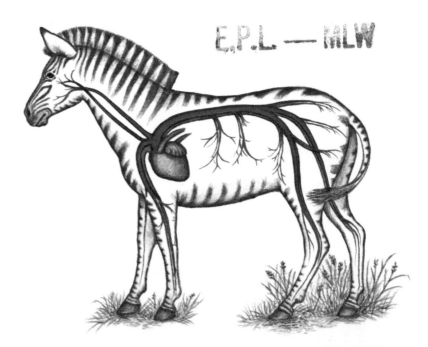

LIFE ON EARTH:
Biology Today

BY Donald M. Silver, PH.D.

ILLUSTRATED BY Patricia J. Wynne

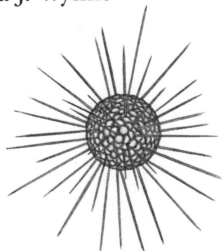

 RANDOM HOUSE

NEW YORK

For Jeanette and Will,
who made this possible.

I would like to thank Patricia J. Wynne for illustrations that make this book come alive. The quality of her mind matches the brilliance of her art. Thanks also to Dr. Guy Musser of the American Museum of Natural History for his expert comments about life on Earth and to Anne Christensen for her expert handling of this book from beginning to end. I am especially grateful to Thomas L. Cathey for donating his time to reading and improving my work.

Donald M. Silver, Ph.D.
March, 1983

Library of Congress Cataloging in Publication Data:
Silver, Donald M.
  Life on earth.
  Includes index.
  SUMMARY: A basic explanation of how plants and animals function and relate to each other.
  1. Biology—Juvenile literature. [1. Biology]
I. Wynne, Patricia, ill. II. Title.
QH309.S54   1983   574   83-4570
ISBN: 0-394-85971-5 (pbk.); 0-394-95971-X (lib. bdg.)

Manufactured in the United States of America

1 2 3 4 5 6 7 8 9 0

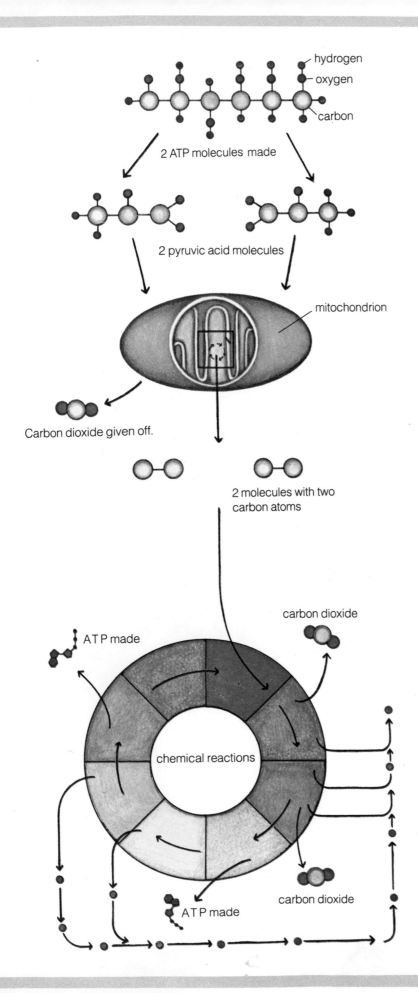

hydrogen
oxygen
carbon

2 ATP molecules made

2 pyruvic acid molecules

mitochondrion

Carbon dioxide given off.

2 molecules with two carbon atoms

carbon dioxide

ATP made

chemical reactions

carbon dioxide

ATP made

CONTENTS

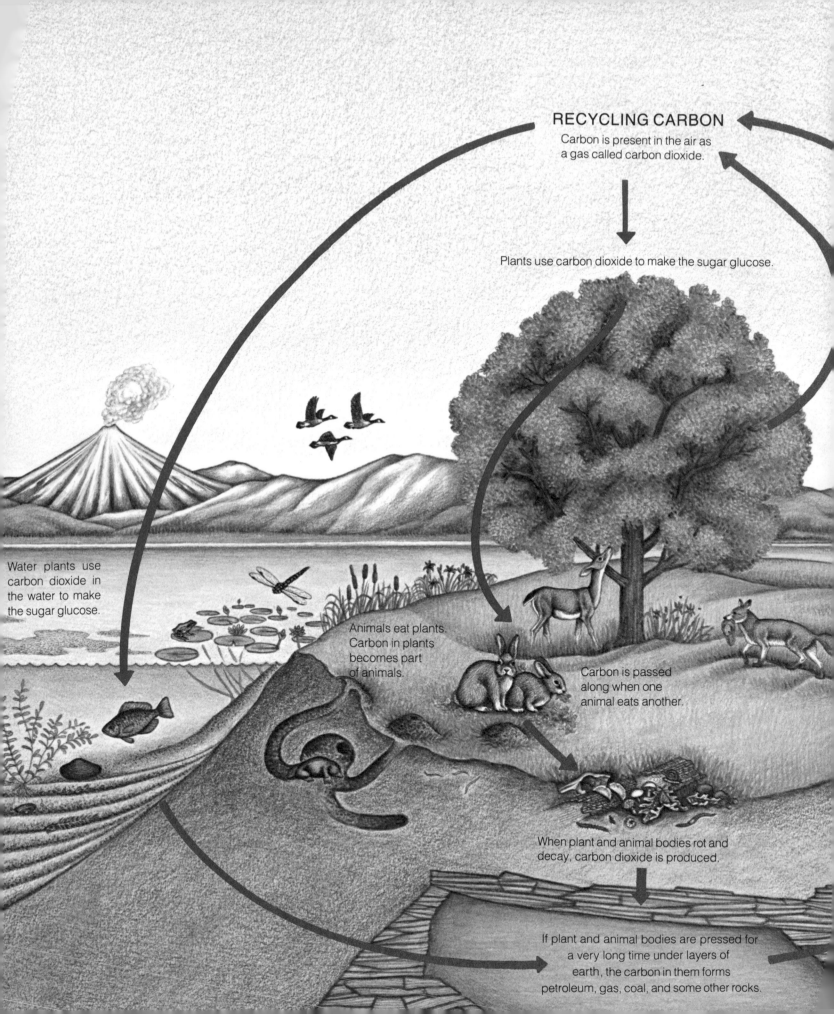

RECYCLING CARBON

Carbon is present in the air as a gas called carbon dioxide.

Plants use carbon dioxide to make the sugar glucose.

Water plants use carbon dioxide in the water to make the sugar glucose.

Animals eat plants. Carbon in plants becomes part of animals.

Carbon is passed along when one animal eats another.

When plant and animal bodies rot and decay, carbon dioxide is produced.

If plant and animal bodies are pressed for a very long time under layers of earth, the carbon in them forms petroleum, gas, coal, and some other rocks.

The carbon cycle shows how living things use and reuse the element carbon. It is called a cycle because all of the stages in it are repeated again and again.

All living things contain carbon. On land and in the water, green plants take in carbon dioxide and use it to make a sugar called glucose (red arrows). Sugar is food for plants and animals. The purple arrows show how carbon returns as carbon dioxide to the air and water to be reused by living things.

Every time fuels are burned, carbon dioxide escapes into the air.

Every time animals and plants breathe, carbon dioxide is given off.

Life on Earth

E arth is full of living things. Some you see everyday, like birds, trees, and your pets. But these are only a few of the more than a million kinds of living things found on Earth. Some creatures, such as polar bears, live where many people never have a chance to visit. Others, like bacteria, are so tiny that you can see them only through a microscope.

This book is about all living things and what they have in common. It will explain to you why plants and animals need each other. And it will introduce you to some of the wonderful creatures that make up life on Earth. All of the materials necessary for life are found on Earth. These materials include air, water, food, and minerals. The heat and light needed by living things come to Earth from the Sun.

Earth's resources are made up of 92 different kinds of simple substances called elements. When living things grow, they use these elements to build the different parts of their bodies. Just six of these elements make up 99 percent of every living thing. These six are hydrogen, oxygen, carbon, nitrogen, phosphorus, and sulfur. Since there is only a limited amount of each element found on Earth, living things have to keep reusing these elements so that the supply of each one never runs out.

The Carbon Cycle

The element called carbon is an important part of every living thing. It is also found in some nonliving things, such as limestone and coal. In air and water, carbon is present as a gas called carbon dioxide.

Green plants take in carbon dioxide and use it to produce a sugar called glucose (the red arrows). Plants need sugar for energy and to make leaves, stems, and roots. When animals eat plants, the carbon in the plants is reused by the animals to develop healthy bodies. Whenever one animal eats another, the carbon is passed along.

If green plants kept taking carbon dioxide out of the air and water, they would eventually use up the entire supply. But this doesn't happen. By following the purple arrows, you can find out the different ways carbon dioxide is put back into the air and water.

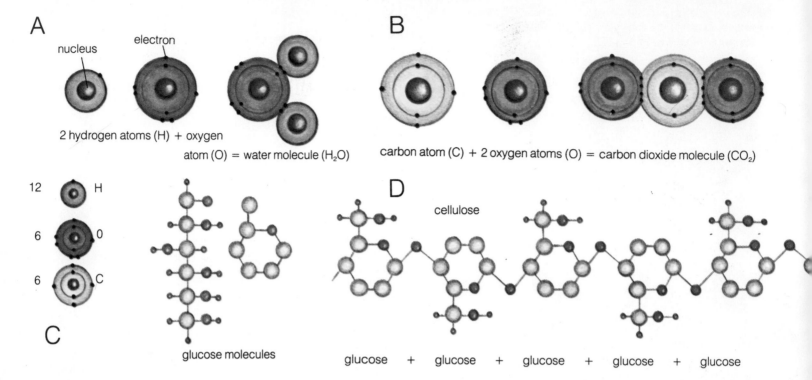

A

nucleus   electron

2 hydrogen atoms (H) + oxygen
atom (O) = water molecule (H$_2$O)

B

carbon atom (C) + 2 oxygen atoms (O) = carbon dioxide molecule (CO$_2$)

12   H

6   O

6   C

C

glucose molecules

D

cellulose

glucose + glucose + glucose + glucose + glucose

ATOMS AND MOLECULES Elements are made of atoms. Each atom has a nucleus. Circling the nucleus are electrons. Atoms form bonds by sharing electrons. Water (A) and carbon dioxide (B) consist of atoms sharing electrons. A molecule of the sugar glucose (C) has many atoms. When glucose is dissolved in water, its atoms form a closed ring. Long chains of glucose molecules make cellulose (D).

As you can see, carbon cycles back and forth between living and nonliving things. But no matter what route it takes, it returns as carbon dioxide to the water and air to be used over and over again by plants and animals.

Atoms and Molecules

Elements are made up of building blocks called atoms. At the center of each atom is its nucleus, which contains most of its weight. Circling the nucleus are tiny particles called electrons. Electrons weigh very little and move extremely quickly as they orbit the nucleus. Because they move so fast, it is almost impossible to tell where an electron is at any moment.

The simplest atom is a hydrogen atom. It has one electron circling its nucleus. A carbon atom has six electrons orbiting its nucleus (see illustration).

Combinations of atoms make up everything found on Earth. When atoms combine, they form bonds with each other. A bond is a force that holds atoms together. Sometimes atoms give electrons to other atoms. This forms a bond called an ionic bond. At-

oms can also share electrons with other atoms. Sharing creates a stronger bond, called a covalent bond.

When two or more atoms join together, they form molecules. The atoms in a molecule can be the same or different. For example, an oxygen molecule consists of two oxygen atoms sharing electrons. Water is produced when two hydrogen atoms share electrons with one oxygen atom. In a molecule of carbon dioxide, one carbon atom combines with two oxygen atoms.

Large molecules are made up of many atoms. For example, glucose, a simple sugar, has six carbon atoms, twelve hydrogen atoms, and six oxygen atoms joined together. The carbon atoms form the backbone of the glucose molecule. All of the other atoms are attached to this backbone. Glucose is the main source of energy for most living things. When the bonds holding the atoms in glucose together are broken, energy is released.

Along with other sugars, glucose is part of a group of substances called carbohydrates. Some carbohydrates, like table sugar, are made up of only a few sugar molecules linked together. Others, like starch and cellulose, consist of hundreds of sugar molecules linked together into long chains. Starch is found in foods like potatoes, and cellulose is the tough, fiber-like material present in plants.

Carbohydrates are not the only large molecules found in all living things. Three other important groups of large molecules are proteins (page 22), fatty substances (page 26), and nucleic acids (page 66).

Molecules are not alive by themselves. Yet when they are assembled together in certain ways, they form the parts that make up living cells.

Animal Cells

Cells are units of living material. The bodies of all living things are formed from cells. Without them, there would be no life. Your body is made of billions of cells that have different sizes and shapes. Practically all cells are too tiny to be seen without a microscope.

Cells contain special structures called organelles. Each organelle has special work to do. This work includes taking in food and breaking it apart into simple molecules, releasing energy from food, building and repairing cell parts, getting rid of harmful wastes, and making more cells.

Cells are enclosed in protective elastic coverings called membranes. Everything entering or leaving a cell must pass through the cell membrane. Most membranes consist of proteins and two layers of fatty substances (page 26).

Inside the membrane, cells are divided into the cytoplasm and the nucleus. The organelles float in the jellylike cytoplasm. Floating is possible because cytoplasm is mostly water. The nucleus controls the

ANIMAL CELL   Cells are units of living material that are divided into a nucleus and cytoplasm. The nucleus controls the activities of the cell. The cytoplasm contains special parts called organelles. Cells are enclosed by elastic coverings called membranes.

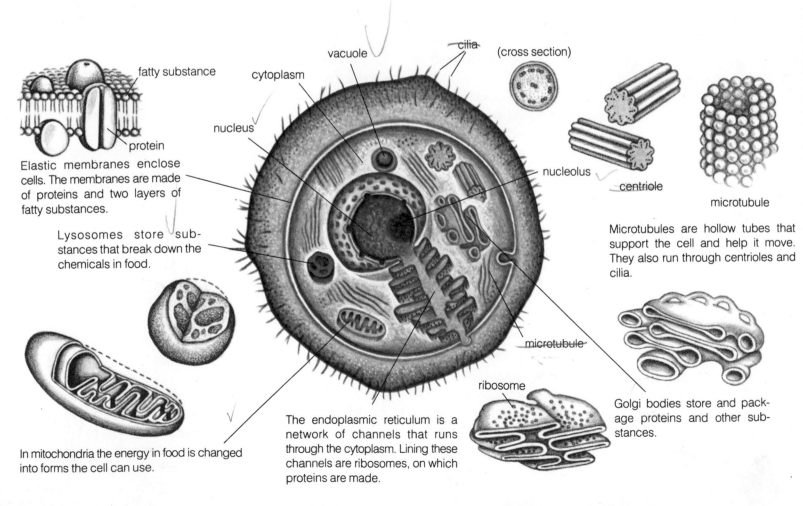

fatty substance

cytoplasm

vacuole

cilia

(cross section)

nucleus

protein

Elastic membranes enclose cells. The membranes are made of proteins and two layers of fatty substances.

Lysosomes store substances that break down the chemicals in food.

nucleolus

centriole

microtubule

Microtubules are hollow tubes that support the cell and help it move. They also run through centrioles and cilia.

microtubule

ribosome

In mitochondria the energy in food is changed into forms the cell can use.

The endoplasmic reticulum is a network of channels that runs through the cytoplasm. Lining these channels are ribosomes, on which proteins are made.

Golgi bodies store and package proteins and other substances.

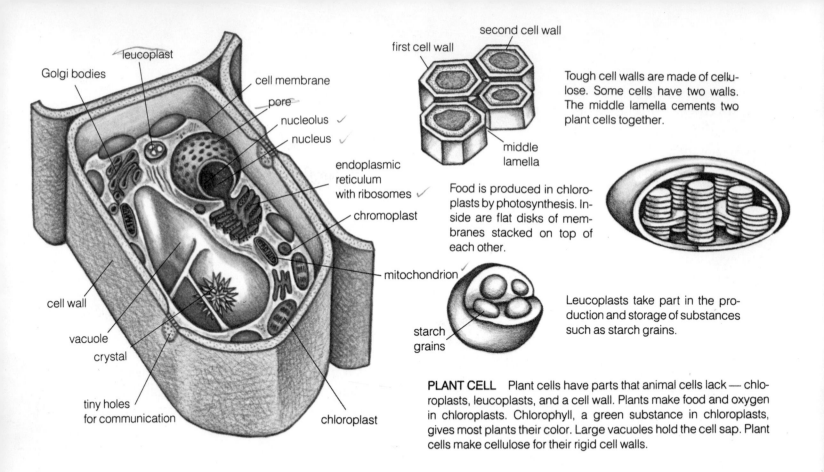

Golgi bodies

leucoplast

cell membrane

pore

nucleolus ✓

nucleus ✓

endoplasmic
reticulum
with ribosomes ✓

chromoplast

cell wall

mitochondrion ✓

vacuole

crystal

tiny holes
for communication

chloroplast

first cell wall

second cell wall

middle
lamella

Tough cell walls are made of cellulose. Some cells have two walls. The middle lamella cements two plant cells together.

Food is produced in chloroplasts by photosynthesis. Inside are flat disks of membranes stacked on top of each other.

starch
grains

Leucoplasts take part in the production and storage of substances such as starch grains.

PLANT CELL Plant cells have parts that animal cells lack — chloroplasts, leucoplasts, and a cell wall. Plants make food and oxygen in chloroplasts. Chlorophyll, a green substance in chloroplasts, gives most plants their color. Large vacuoles hold the cell sap. Plant cells make cellulose for their rigid cell walls.

activities of the cell. Without it a cell could neither grow nor reproduce.

Surrounding the nucleus are two special membranes with a space between them. At various points the inner and outer membranes pinch together, creating pores. These pores are not completely open. Even so, certain molecules can pass through them, allowing communication between the nucleus and the rest of the cell.

Inside the nucleus is a dense area called the nucleolus. Here the cell makes some of the parts it needs for putting together proteins. These parts move out of the nucleus and into the cytoplasm.

Chemical reactions take place in the cytoplasm all the time. Molecules are able to move from one part of the cytoplasm to another through fluid-filled channels known as the endoplasmic reticulum.

In the cytoplasm proteins are put together on small round bodies called ribosomes. This process is explained on page 22. Certain proteins are stored in Golgi bodies, and other proteins are packaged there and released to do work in the cytoplasm.

In order to grow and remain healthy, all cells need energy from food. The energy in foods must be changed into chemical forms the cell can use. This change takes place in sausage-shaped mitochondria and is part of the process of respiration (page 27).

Many cells move around, using the little hairs on their surface. These hairs are made of tiny, hollow tubes called microtubules. Many short hairs beating like oars are called cilia. One, or a few, long hairs whipping back and forth are called flagella. Inside cells, microtubules help to control the shape of a cell and make it strong.

When a cell divides, two new cells are formed. During division, DNA molecules in the nucleus move apart (see page 67). They are helped in this process by two centrioles located just outside of the nucleus. Centrioles are made of microtubules too.

Plant Cells

Plant cells are different from animal cells. In addition to having a nucleus, a cell membrane, and cytoplasm, plant cells have a number of parts not found in animal cells. In one part, called the chloroplast, plant cells produce glucose by the process of photosynthesis (see page 15). Chloroplasts contain a green chemical called chlorophyll. Often each plant cell has many chloroplasts.

If plant cells produce more sugar than they need, they can store it as starch in leucoplasts. Proteins and fatty substances are also stored inside leucoplasts.

Many fruits, flowers, and autumn leaves are not green. The ones that are yellow or orange get their coloring from chemicals made in chromoplasts in their cells.

In other plants, cells have red, blue, or purple chemicals inside large fluid-filled cavities called vacuoles. Vacuoles hold the cell sap, which consists of water, gases, salts, and sugars. Vacuoles frequently become so large that they crowd the other parts of the cell up against the cell membrane.

Just about all plant cells have a rigid cell wall outside of their cell membranes. These tough, thick walls provide extra support for the cell. Cell walls are made of long chains of cellulose. One plant cell can communicate with another through tiny holes in the cell wall.

Cells to Organisms

There are thousands of different kinds of living things that are made up of only a single tiny cell. Some are pictured on this page. Each of these cells is able to carry on all of the work necessary for staying alive. This work includes taking in food and getting rid of harmful wastes.

It is amazing how different each of these cells is. Just like plant cells, three of these single cells (euglena, diatom, and a green alga called chlamydomonas) can produce their own food. The rest have to find their food in the waters where they live.

Sometimes single cells join together to form colonies. Volvox is such a colony and can also make its own food.

Most plants and animals are made up of many cells. But all of these cells are not identical. There are different kinds of cells that do different jobs. In plants, for instance, there are root cells that take in minerals and water from the soil, and leaf cells that produce food. In the same way, human beings use special cells for seeing and other cells for movement.

In most plants and animals, cells are arranged into tissues and organs. Groups of cells that do the same job are called tissues. Muscle tissue, for example, is made up of many individual muscle cells.

Different tissues that work together form organs. Some organs you are already familiar with are your stomach, kidneys, and lungs. More than one organ is usually needed to get a job done. These organs are called a system.

Whether a living thing is made of one cell or many cells, each organism has certain basic needs. One of the most important of these is the need for food.

There are thousands of different kinds of single-celled organisms. A few of them are illustrated below.

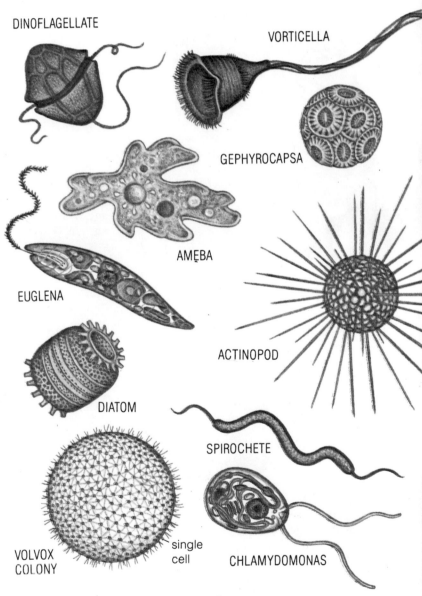

DINOFLAGELLATE

VORTICELLA

GEPHYROCAPSA

AMEBA

EUGLENA

ACTINOPOD

DIATOM

SPIROCHETE

VOLVOX COLONY

single cell

CHLAMYDOMONAS

Volvox is a colony of cells that live together.

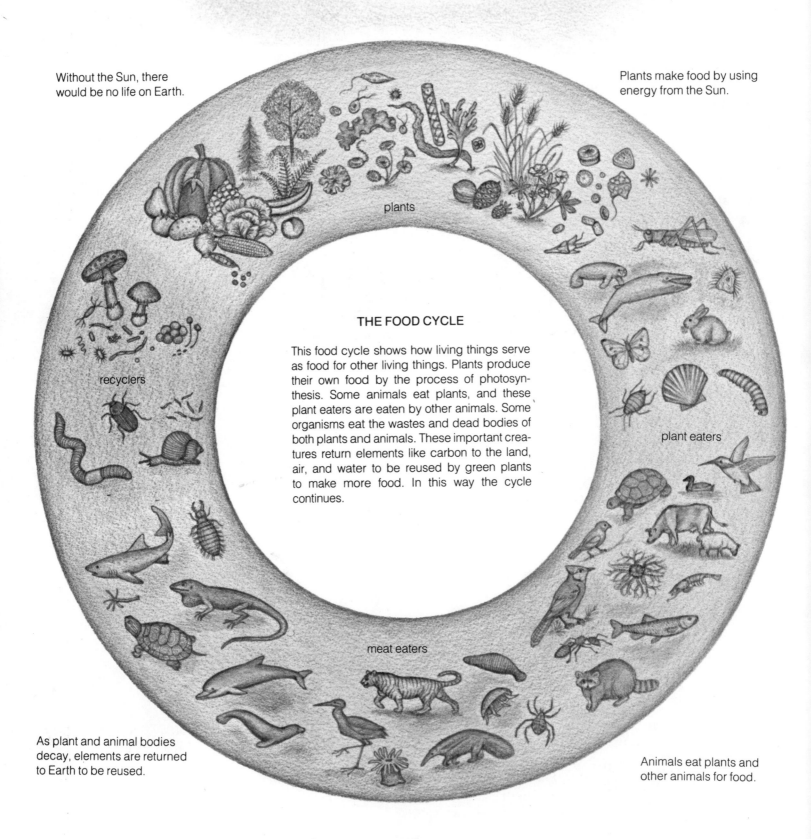

Sun

Without the Sun, there would be no life on Earth.

Plants make food by using energy from the Sun.

plants

recyclers

THE FOOD CYCLE

This food cycle shows how living things serve as food for other living things. Plants produce their own food by the process of photosynthesis. Some animals eat plants, and these plant eaters are eaten by other animals. Some organisms eat the wastes and dead bodies of both plants and animals. These important creatures return elements like carbon to the land, air, and water to be reused by green plants to make more food. In this way the cycle continues.

plant eaters

meat eaters

As plant and animal bodies decay, elements are returned to Earth to be reused.

Animals eat plants and other animals for food.

The Need for Food

Just as a machine needs energy to run, the parts of a cell constantly need energy to perform their different jobs. There are many forms of energy: heat, light, sound, electrical, and chemical. Chemical energy is the one that cells can use.

Food supplies plants and animals with energy. Energy is stored in the molecules in food. The most common source of energy is glucose.

Food also provides cells with six types of building blocks, called nutrients. These six nutrients are carbohydrates, proteins, fats, vitamins, minerals, and water. Carbohydrates, proteins, and fats are all sources of energy and of the building materials cells must have to grow. Minerals and vitamins are needed for the chemical activities carried on inside the cells. Cells use only tiny amounts of vitamins. And they usually need much more of some minerals, like sodium, than others, like copper. Water is found in every cell. It makes up about 75 percent of your body. Water also takes part in chemical reactions.

The Food Cycle

Most living things eat other living things as food. The ways in which one organism serves as food for another are shown in the illustration of the food cycle.

Green plants are at the top of the circle because they produce their own food. If you move clockwise around the circle, you will find some animals that eat plants.

Microscopic plants, called algae, are found in waters all over the world. Algae are eaten by microscopic animals. Billions of these tiny floating plants and animals are referred to as plankton. Plankton is food for small fish and even for some large animals, like whales.

The blue area of the circle shows some animals that eat other animals for food. Usually, small animals are eaten by larger ones. Some animals, such as raccoons and humans, eat both plants and other animals.

All living things eventually die. Continue around the circle to the gray area and you will find the creatures that eat the wastes and dead bodies of animals and plants. These creatures break down dead bodies into simple substances that are returned to Earth to be used by other living things. One of these substances, carbon dioxide, is reused by plants to make more food.

Energy from the Sun

Green plants get the energy they need to make food from the Sun. Plant cells change the energy in sunlight into chemical energy and store it in molecules called ATP (adenosine triphosphate). ATP carries chemical energy to the places where glucose is produced.

ATP

Every molecule of ATP contains three phosphorus atoms linked together in a chain. Chemical energy is stored in the phosphate bonds holding these phosphorus atoms together. When energy is needed in a cell, the last phosphate bond is broken. If more energy is needed, the middle bond is broken. When the bonds break, energy is released. Like batteries, ATP molecules can be recharged after they lose their energy. They recharge by picking up more chemical energy and re-forming the phosphate bonds. Both plant and animal cells use ATP to store and carry energy.

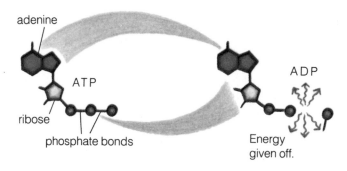

ENERGY FOR LIFE ATP is used by all living things to store, carry, and transfer energy. It has three phosphorus atoms bonded together. Energy is stored in these phosphate bonds. When energy is needed, the last bond is broken and ATP becomes ADP (adenosine diphosphate). Like a battery, ATP can be recharged if ADP picks up more energy and re-forms the broken bond.

Sun

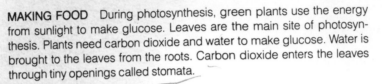

MAKING FOOD During photosynthesis, green plants use the energy from sunlight to make glucose. Leaves are the main site of photosynthesis. Plants need carbon dioxide and water to make glucose. Water is brought to the leaves from the roots. Carbon dioxide enters the leaves through tiny openings called stomata.

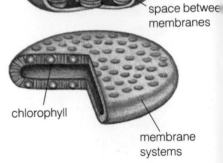

chloroplast

space betwee membranes

chlorophyll

membrane systems

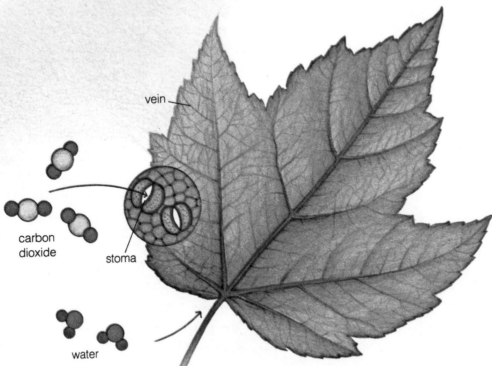

vein

carbon dioxide

stoma

water

Glucose is made only in cells containing chlorophyll. Chlorophyll is found in chloroplasts on systems of membranes. Here, light energy is captured and changed into chemical energy. The chemical energy is used to produce glucose in the space between the membranes.

Photosynthesis

Green plants manufacture food by a process called photosynthesis. They capture light energy from the Sun and change it into chemical energy. This energy, carried by ATP, is used to put together glucose molecules. Without plants there would be no food, and without the Sun, no life on Earth.

Sunlight consists of particles called photons. Each photon is a package of energy waves. You can see the different energy waves in the colors of the rainbow.

Photosynthesis takes place mainly in a plant's leaves. Leaves are so thin that no plant cell lies far from the surface. When sunlight hits the surface of a leaf, energy is absorbed by plant cells and captured by chlorophyll molecules.

Glucose is produced only in cells containing chlorophyll. In most plant cells, chlorophyll is present on systems of membranes inside chloroplasts.

Glucose is made of carbon, oxygen, and hydrogen atoms (page 8). For plants to produce glucose, they need a supply of all of these atoms. Carbon dioxide provides the carbon and oxygen atoms. It enters the leaves through tiny openings called stomata. Most stomata open only during the day when the Sun is shining.

The hydrogen atoms needed to make glucose come from water. Water is carried up from the plant's roots to its leaves. All plant cells are bathed in water.

The process of photosynthesis is illustrated on the opposite page. During photosynthesis, hydrogen atoms are taken away from water molecules. This breaks up the water molecules and frees the oxygen, which escapes into the air. Animals and plants need a constant supply of oxygen for respiration (page 27). Under water, plants carrying on photosynthesis give off oxygen into the water.

All over the world plants are producing food and giving off oxygen. As long as they continue to do this, the supply of food and oxygen will never run out.

HOW PHOTOSYNTHESIS WORKS Plants produce glucose by photosynthesis. To do this they need carbon, oxygen, and hydrogen atoms. And they also need energy. The diagram below represents inside a leaf.

1. When the Sun shines, leaf cells absorb sunlight. Inside chloroplasts, electrons in chlorophyll molecules soak up so much energy from sunlight that they "pop out" of their molecules. Every chlorophyll molecule that loses an electron is no longer complete. To become complete again, each one takes an electron from a water molecule.

2. When an electron is taken away from a water molecule, water breaks up into hydrogen and oxygen. The oxygen escapes into the air and you breathe some of it in. The hydrogen remains and is used to make glucose.

3. The energy in the "popped-out" electron is used to make ATP. Light energy becomes chemical energy, which the cell can use.

4. Carbon dioxide from the air enters leaves when the stomata are open. It supplies the carbon and oxygen atoms needed to make glucose.

5. By a series of chemical reactions, glucose is produced. These reactions are driven by the energy released from the ATP molecules. When ATP loses energy, the ADP that remains returns to step 3 to be recharged. Since the cell is using chemical energy, this part of the process can take place in the dark.

6. Plant cells use glucose to make cellulose and fats. Some glucose is transported to cells that need energy, such as root cells. Glucose that is not used can be stored as starch.

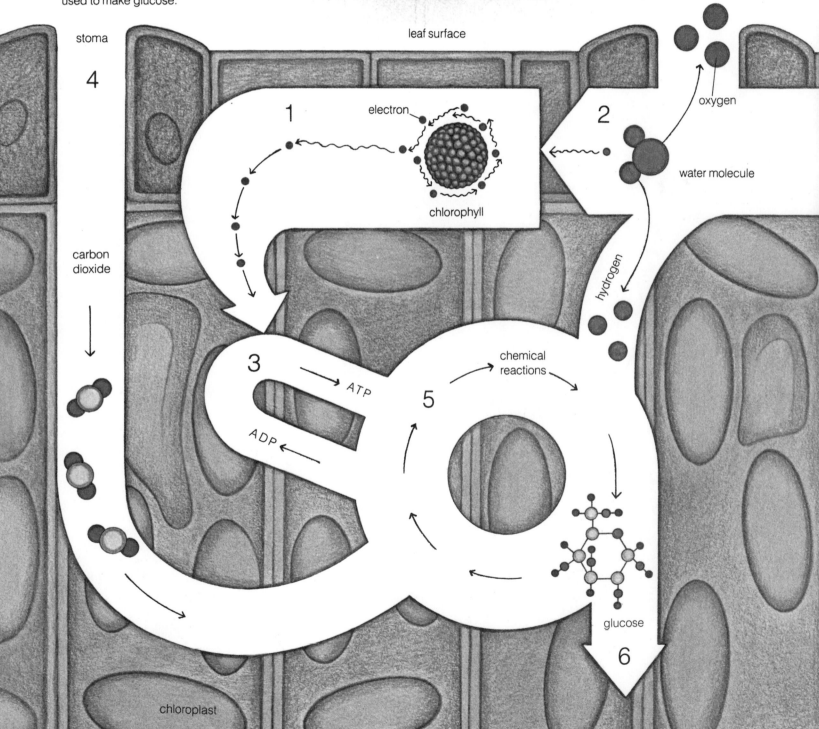

Sun

stoma

leaf surface

4

1

electron

chlorophyll

2

oxygen

water molecule

carbon dioxide

hydrogen

3

ATP

ADP

5

chemical reactions

glucose

6

chloroplast

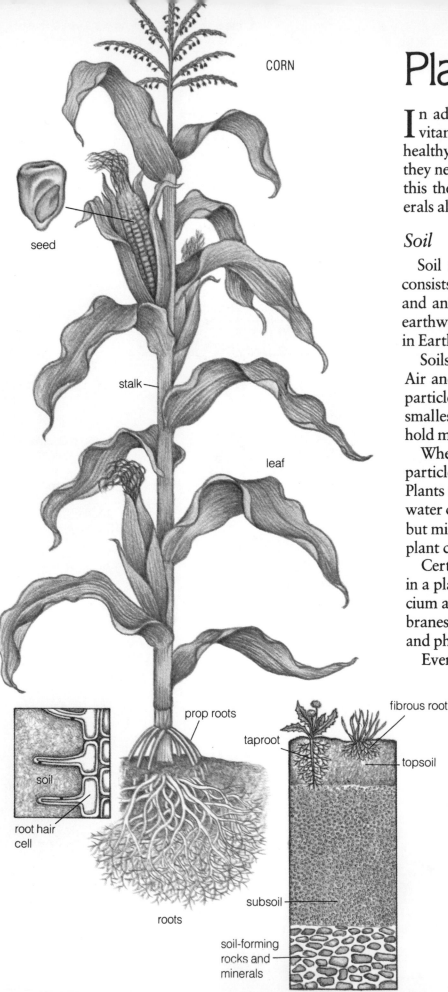

CORN

seed

stalk

leaf

prop roots

soil

root hair
cell

roots

taproot

fibrous root

topsoil

subsoil

soil-forming
rocks and
minerals

Plant Nutrition

In addition to glucose, plants need proteins, fats, vitamins, minerals, and water to grow and stay healthy. Plant cells can make the fats and vitamins they need. They can also produce proteins, but to do this they need nitrogen. Nitrogen, water, and minerals all have to be taken in from the soil.

Soil

Soil makes up the top layer of Earth's crust. It consists of rocks, mineral particles, decayed plant and animal matter, water, and air. Bacteria, fungi, earthworms, insects, and burrowing animals all live in Earth's rich soil.

Soils are made up of different kinds of particles. Air and water are trapped in spaces between these particles. The largest particles in soil are sand; the smallest are clay. Clays help give soil the ability to hold minerals and water.

When water is trapped in the spaces between soil particles, it forms a liquid film around each particle. Plants need water for photosynthesis. Not only does water carry food from one part of a plant to another, but minerals must dissolve in water in order to reach plant cells.

Certain minerals are taken out of the soil by cells in a plant's roots. Plants need large quantities of calcium and potassium for making cell walls and membranes. Magnesium is used for making chlorophyll, and phosphorus is needed for ATP.

Even though nitrogen makes up 78 percent of the

ROOT SYSTEMS There are two major root systems in plants. Taproot systems have one main root, and fibrous root systems have several main roots. In both taproots and fibrous roots, small roots branch from large ones. Water and minerals are absorbed from the soil through millions of tiny root hair cells. Some plants, like corn, have additional roots that develop from the stalk. These are called prop roots and help plants stand up against the wind.

In the illustration on the right, the colored areas show where plants store food.

air, plants cannot use nitrogen in that form. Bacteria in the soil must change this nitrogen into nitrates, a form that plants can use. Some of these bacteria live on the roots of plants like peas and beans. Other kinds of bacteria in the soil produce nitrates from dead plant and animal matter.

Roots

Roots anchor plants in soil. Special root cells take in water and minerals through tiny, very thin root hairs. Plants have tremendous numbers of root hairs. In some plants a hundred million new root hairs develop every day. Roots must grow continually to insure that plants have enough water and minerals. This constant growth requires a steady supply of energy.

Root cells don't have chloroplasts or chlorophyll, so they can't make their own food. Glucose travels from the leaves down into the roots to provide needed energy. To release the energy stored in the glucose molecules, root cells need the oxygen in the air that is trapped between soil particles. If there is too much water in the soil, the air is forced out and the root cells die.

There are two major types of root systems. Many garden plants and grasses have several main roots in what is called a fibrous root system. Lots of small roots branch out from these main roots. In a taproot system, however, which is found in most trees and some plants, such as carrots, there is only one main root, called a taproot. Side roots branch out from the taproot. Some roots extend 12 feet (4 meters) down into the ground. Others stay near the surface, extending over a large area.

Storing Food

When plants produce more sugar than they need, they change it into starch and store it. For trees and plants that lose their leaves in winter, stored food serves as a source of energy until new leaves grow in the spring.

The illustration at the bottom of this page shows where different types of plants store their food. Food is stored in the leaves of the cabbage plant, the flowers of the cauliflower plant, and the stem of the celery plant. Violets store food in underground stems called rhizomes. Some rhizomes have enlarged end portions, or tubers. Potatoes are tubers filled with starch. The onions you eat are short underground stems surrounded by thick, colorless leaves.

Roots can also become filled with stored food. Carrots, beets, and turnips are all taproots filled with food.

Many plants grow from seeds. Plants store food in their seeds so that each young plant will have a supply of energy until its leaves develop and it can make food for itself. Peas, beans, and grains like wheat, barley, and rye are all seeds.

Seeds are usually protected by fruits. Eggplants, pumpkins, tomatoes, and squash, as well as apples and oranges, are fruits that protect the seeds inside them.

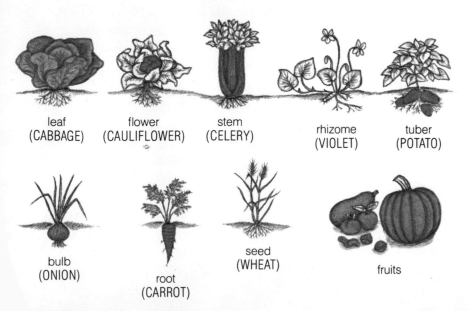

leaf (CABBAGE)

flower (CAULIFLOWER)

stem (CELERY)

rhizome (VIOLET)

tuber (POTATO)

bulb (ONION)

root (CARROT)

seed (WHEAT)

fruits

Some plants growing in mineral-poor soil must get their nutrients from other sources. The Venus's-flytrap is one of the few kinds of animal-eating plants. Its leaves attract insects. If an insect lands on a leaf and touches sensitive hairs, the leaf closes around it and it becomes trapped. The plant then gives off chemicals that digest the insect. Minerals and nutrients from the insect are absorbed by the plant.

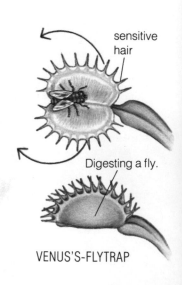

sensitive hair

Digesting a fly.

VENUS'S-FLYTRAP

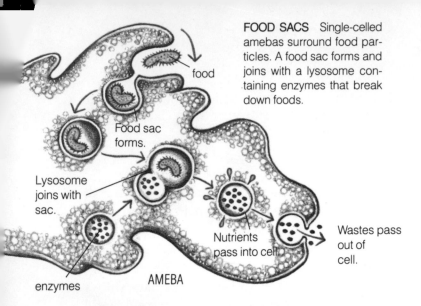

FOOD SACS Single-celled amebas surround food particles. A food sac forms and joins with a lysosome containing enzymes that break down foods.

food

Food sac forms.

Lysosome joins with sac.

enzymes

Nutrients pass into cell.

Wastes pass out of cell.

AMEBA

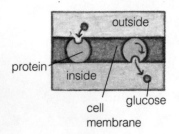

ACTIVE TRANSPORT After the molecules in food are broken apart, they are small enough to get through cell membranes. Membrane proteins pick up nutrients outside of cells and bring them inside.

outside

protein

inside

glucose

cell membrane

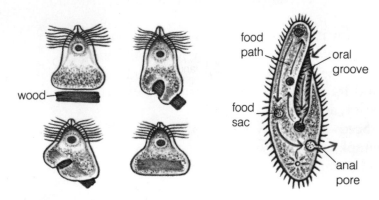

PARAMECIUM

wood

food path

oral groove

food sac

anal pore

DIGESTION IN SINGLE CELLS Single-celled organisms (above left) live in a termite's digestive system and help it to digest plant cells in wood. A paramecium (above right) has an oral groove to take in food and an anal pore to get rid of wastes.

SIMPLE DIGESTIVE SYSTEMS Animals such as hydras have tentacles with stingers that paralyze tiny floating animals. The tentacles draw food into the mouth. Digestion by enzymes takes place in the jelly-filled central sac.

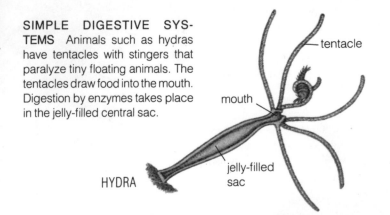

tentacle

mouth

jelly-filled sac

HYDRA

Digestion

Unlike plants, animals can't produce their own food. They have to find food and get it to every cell in their bodies. Usually the carbohydrate, protein, and fat molecules in foods are too big to get through the membranes surrounding animal cells. The process of digestion breaks them apart into small molecules that can get through cell membranes.

Food is digested with the help of enzymes, which are proteins that speed up chemical reactions. Digestive enzymes attach to molecules in food and break apart the bonds holding them together. When you eat potatoes, digestive enzymes break apart starch molecules into glucose molecules. Glucose molecules are small enough to be transported into your cells. In order for most enzymes to work properly, vitamins must be present in cells.

Finding Food

Every animal has its own way of capturing food. In water, single-celled amebas move along until they find food particles. As they move, amebas change their body shape. When they find food, part of their body surrounds it, forming a food sac. This sac travels around inside the ameba until it joins up with a lysosome — a floating package containing digestive enzymes. These enzymes break the food particles into small molecules the ameba can use. Undigested materials remain in the sac until the sac reaches a spot where the membrane opens and wastes are eliminated.

Hydras are simple animals made up of many cells. They use their tentacles to feel around in the water for food. Tiny stingers on their tentacles can paralyze small floating animals. After food is captured, it is drawn by the tentacles into the hydra's mouth. From there it moves down into a jelly-filled sac where digestive enzymes are given off. As the food molecules break apart, they are absorbed by some of the cells lining the sac. Digestion is completed inside of these cells. Undigested wastes return to the mouth, where they are eliminated.

In most animals digestion takes place in a long tube with openings at both ends. This tube is divided into sections, or organs, that do different jobs. All of

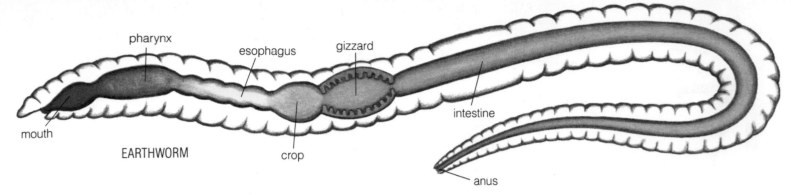

EARTHWORM
mouth · pharynx · esophagus · gizzard · crop · intestine · anus

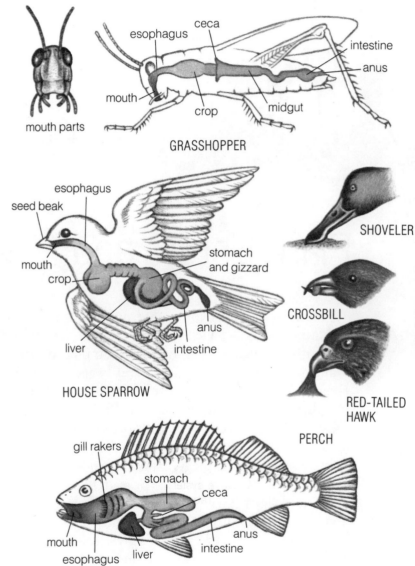

GRASSHOPPER
mouth parts · mouth · esophagus · ceca · crop · midgut · intestine · anus

HOUSE SPARROW
seed beak · esophagus · mouth · crop · liver · stomach and gizzard · anus · intestine

SHOVELER

CROSSBILL

RED-TAILED HAWK

PERCH
gill rakers · mouth · esophagus · stomach · liver · ceca · intestine · anus

the organs doing the work of digesting food make up the digestive system. As if on a one-way street, food travels in only one direction through the tube.

Earthworms are good examples of this tubelike digestive system. When an earthworm burrows underground, it sucks soil containing food into its mouth. From the mouth, this mixture is moistened as it moves through a connecting tube into a storage area called the crop. Next it enters the muscular gizzard, where tiny particles of sand help grind it up. Then the partially digested mixture passes into the long intestine. Here digestion is completed by enzymes, and nutrients are absorbed into the earthworm's body. At the end of the tube undigested wastes and soil particles are eliminated through the anus. These wastes are deposited on Earth's surface. Earthworms benefit the soil because they mix and loosen it, creating spaces for air and water.

If you compare the digestive systems in the animals shown on this page, you will see how basically similar they are. But insects such as grasshoppers have special mouth parts for tasting, biting, and grinding food. Birds have many kinds of strong, hard beaks for handling a wide variety of foods, ranging from seeds to fish. Seed-eating birds use their beaks to crack open seeds. These seeds are stored in the crop until they move into the stomach. In the first part of the stomach the seeds are mixed with digestive juices. The second part, the muscular gizzard, has ridges that crush and grind the seeds. Some birds, like finches, swallow small rocks to make this grinding easier. Digestion is completed in the small intestine with the help of fluids from the liver and pancreas.

Many fish have rakelike parts in their gills that filter food particles out of the water. Other fish, like sharks, have rows of teeth that tear off chunks from the animals they eat.

DIGESTION IN ANIMALS In most animals digestion takes place in a long tube. In earthworms food enters the mouth and is stored in the crop, ground up in the gizzard, and chemically broken down in the intestines. Wastes pass out through the anus. Grasshoppers have special mouth parts for biting and tasting food. They also have ceca, small pouches in the intestines that give off digestive enzymes. Birds use their bills and beaks to capture fish and open seeds. As water flows over the gills of many fish, gill rakers filter out food.

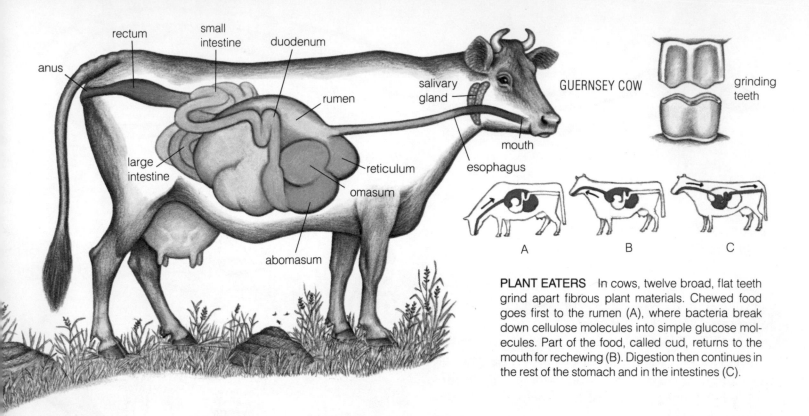

anus
rectum
small intestine
duodenum
rumen
salivary gland
GUERNSEY COW
grinding teeth
mouth
large intestine
reticulum
esophagus
omasum
abomasum

A   B   C

PLANT EATERS In cows, twelve broad, flat teeth grind apart fibrous plant materials. Chewed food goes first to the rumen (A), where bacteria break down cellulose molecules into simple glucose molecules. Part of the food, called cud, returns to the mouth for rechewing (B). Digestion then continues in the rest of the stomach and in the intestines (C).

Plant Eaters and Meat Eaters

Animals eat plants and other animals for food. Some animals, such as cows, horses, and rabbits, are called herbivores, because their diet consists mainly of plants. Lions, dogs, and bears are meat eaters, or carnivores. Carnivores have to capture and kill their food. Although you eat both plants and meat, your digestive system is more like a lion's than a cow's.

In plant eaters and meat eaters, digestion begins in the mouth. Cows have broad, flat teeth that grind up grass, and lions have sharp, pointed teeth that cut and tear into their prey. Salivary glands in the mouth give off a digestive juice called saliva. Saliva softens and moistens food. It also contains an enzyme that starts changing starch into sugar. Often, just the sight or smell of food is enough to start the flow of saliva.

In the mouth food is chewed into pieces, mixed with saliva, and chewed some more. Then the tongue moves it to the back of the mouth, where it is swallowed. Swallowing takes place in a muscular tube called the esophagus. Food is squeezed along to the stomach by a rippling motion called peristalsis.

Digestion in the Stomach

A cow's stomach has four chambers. Swallowed food empties into the rumen, a chamber that can hold 25 to 60 gallons (95 to 230 liters) of food. There are large numbers of bacteria and other microorganisms in the rumen. These organisms produce enzymes that split cellulose molecules into simple glucose molecules (page 8). Cows could not break down the tough, fiberlike cellulose in plant cell walls without the help of these organisms.

Plant cells are so difficult to digest that from time to time, part of the food in the rumen returns to the cow's mouth for further chewing. This rechewed food, or cud, is swallowed again. But this time it goes into the second and third chambers of the stomach, called the reticulum and omasum. In these chambers water is squeezed out of the food, making it ready for digestion in the fourth chamber, the abomasum. The abomasum is like the stomach of a meat-eating lion.

In the lion's stomach, hydrochloric acid and enzymes pour onto the food. Hydrochloric acid de-

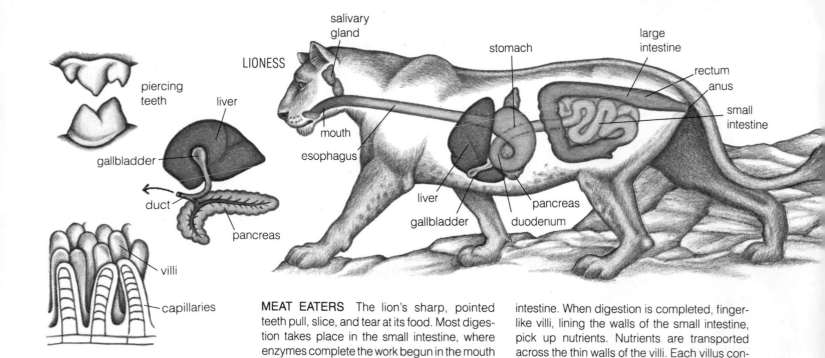

piercing teeth

liver

gallbladder

duct

pancreas

villi

capillaries

salivary gland

LIONESS

mouth

esophagus

stomach

large intestine

rectum

anus

small intestine

liver

gallbladder

pancreas

duodenum

MEAT EATERS The lion's sharp, pointed teeth pull, slice, and tear at its food. Most digestion takes place in the small intestine, where enzymes complete the work begun in the mouth and stomach. Enzymes from the pancreas and bile from the liver enter the first part of the small intestine. When digestion is completed, fingerlike villi, lining the walls of the small intestine, pick up nutrients. Nutrients are transported across the thin walls of the villi. Each villus consists of a network of blood vessels and a lymph vessel.

stroys bacteria and helps enzymes to work properly. One of these enzymes, pepsin, starts digesting proteins. The stomach expands and contracts, mixing food with these digestive juices and mashing up any pieces that remain.

Completing Digestion

In both meat eaters and plant eaters, most digestion takes place in the small intestine. From the stomach, partially digested food slowly enters the first part of the small intestine, called the duodenum. Many different enzymes pour onto it there. Some of these enzymes come from a large gland called the pancreas. The rest are given off by millions of cells in the wall of the intestine. A thick fluid called bile comes from the liver to aid in digestion by making fats dissolve in water. In the liver, bile is stored in the gallbladder until it is needed.

Digestion continues in the rest of the small intestine until carbohydrates, proteins, and fats are broken apart into molecules small enough to pass through the intestinal wall into the body. This absorption takes place in tiny, wiggling, fingerlike parts

called villi, which jut out from the wall of the intestine. Running through each villus are blood vessels called capillaries, which pick up the digested sugars and proteins. Digested fats pass into lymph vessels (page 35). Water, vitamins, and minerals are also absorbed into the bloodstream. Blood carries absorbed nutrients to the liver, where some of them are processed and others are stored.

Undigested materials move by peristalsis into the large intestine, where needed chemicals and more water are absorbed. As this takes place, the liquid materials slowly solidify. These undigested wastes, or feces, are stored in the rectum, the end portion of the large intestine, until they are passed out of the body through the anus.

In some plant eaters, such as horses and rabbits, the organisms that help digest cellulose are not found in the stomach. Instead, they live in a sac located near the beginning of the large intestine.

Unlike plant eaters, you can't digest the cellulose in the plant foods you eat. But this fiber is a very important part of your diet, because before it passes out of your body it provides materials that help your large intestine work smoothly.

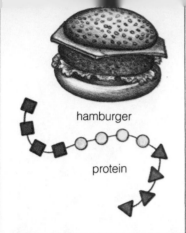

hamburger

protein

1. When you eat a hamburger, you take in proteins. The protein shown here consists of 12 amino acids linked together. Each shape is a different type of amino acid. In this protein there are only three kinds of amino acids.

Making Proteins

Proteins are a very important part of every cell in your body. Proteins are in the nucleus, the cytoplasm, and the cell membrane. Enzymes are proteins. So are some hormones (page 48). And antibodies (page 35), which protect you against harmful bacteria and viruses, are proteins too. Your muscles, hair, skin, and blood contain proteins.

Your body can make, or synthesize, thousands of different proteins. Each protein is made up of amino acids, which are linked together in a chain. Some proteins consist of only a few amino acids, and others are made up of hundreds of amino acids.

Every amino acid has carbon, hydrogen, oxygen, and nitrogen atoms. Some also have sulfur atoms. There are 20 different kinds of amino acids. In the same way that you make short and long words from combinations of the 26 letters of the alphabet, your cells make small and large proteins from combinations of these 20 different amino acids.

When you eat foods such as eggs, fish, and meat, you take in animal proteins. Although you can't use these proteins as they are, you can use the amino acids in food to make your own proteins.

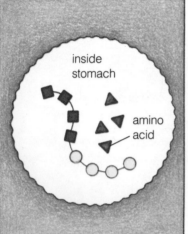

inside stomach

amino acid

2. After you chew and swallow the hamburger, it reaches your stomach. An enzyme called pepsin begins to break the protein apart. The rest of the protein is split apart into amino acids in your small intestine.

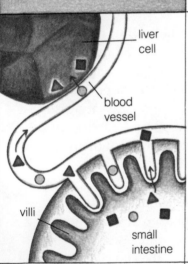

liver cell

blood vessel

villi

small intestine

3. The 12 amino acids pass through the wall of your small intestine into your bloodstream. Your blood carries amino acids first to your liver, then to all the cells in your body. Your liver cells take in all of the amino acids they need.

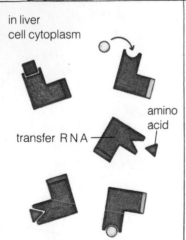

in liver cell cytoplasm

amino acid

transfer RNA

4. Inside each cell are molecules of transfer RNA (ribonucleic acid) that pick up the amino acids. Each kind of amino acid has its own kind of RNA molecule that picks it up. (This is shown by the matching colors in the illustration.) Once the amino acids are attached to their RNA molecules, they move toward the ribosomes. Proteins are put together on ribosomes. Each ribosome consists of one large sphere and one small sphere. Parts for ribosomes are made in the nucleolus. Ribosomes produce proteins by using blueprints that come from the nucleus. Step 5 takes you inside the nucleus.

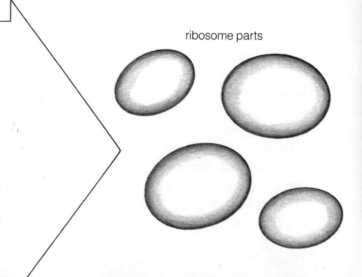

ribosome parts

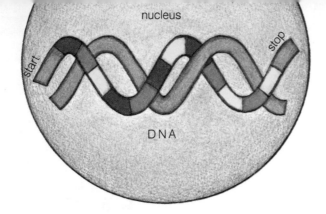

nucleus

DNA

5. In the nucleus of every cell in your body are molecules of DNA (deoxyribonucleic acid; page 66), which contain the blueprints for making all of the proteins you need. This information is in a chemical code. Here the code is shown by the colors. Each color represents the code for a different type of amino acid.

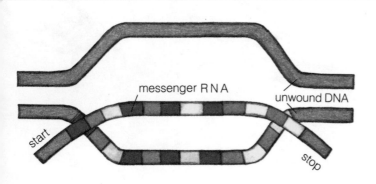

messenger RNA

unwound DNA

start

stop

6. Part of the DNA unwinds. The coded blueprint is copied onto a different type of RNA molecule. This RNA serves as a messenger, carrying the information out of the nucleus to the ribosomes in the cytoplasm. For this reason it is called messenger RNA.

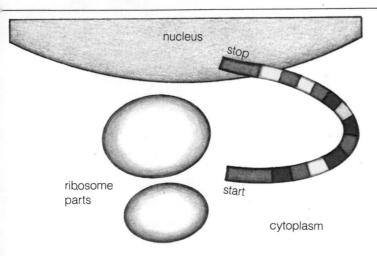

nucleus

stop

ribosome parts

start

cytoplasm

7. There is a "start" signal coded in the messenger RNA that indicates where to begin making the protein. The spheres that make up each ribosome attach to the messenger at "start." First the bottom sphere attaches, then the top joins on.

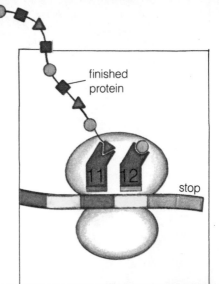

finished protein

stop

11. The process repeats itself. Amino acids are added to the growing chain one at a time. At the end of the messenger is a "stop" signal. The finished protein is released, the ribosome separates, and the two spheres fall off. In this way your body uses amino acids in food to make the proteins you need. Although some proteins remain as straight chains, most fold up into complicated shapes.

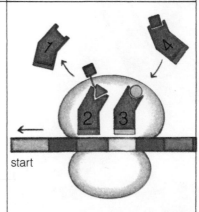

start

10. Amino acids 1 and 2 are linked together by special enzymes. Both amino acids are now attached to the second transfer RNA. The ribosome moves again. As it does, the first transfer RNA leaves the ribosome and the third lands in place. Amino acids 1 and 2 are then linked to amino acid 3.

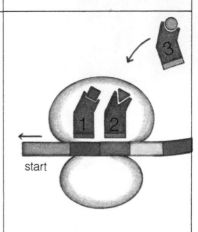

start

9. The ribosome moves again until the code for the second amino acid is in place. The second transfer RNA lands. It carries amino acid 2 for the new protein.

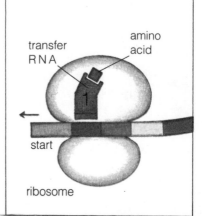

transfer RNA

amino acid

start

ribosome

8. The ribosome moves along the messenger RNA until the code for the first amino acid in the new protein is in place. The transfer RNA matching that code lands on that spot. It carries amino acid 1.

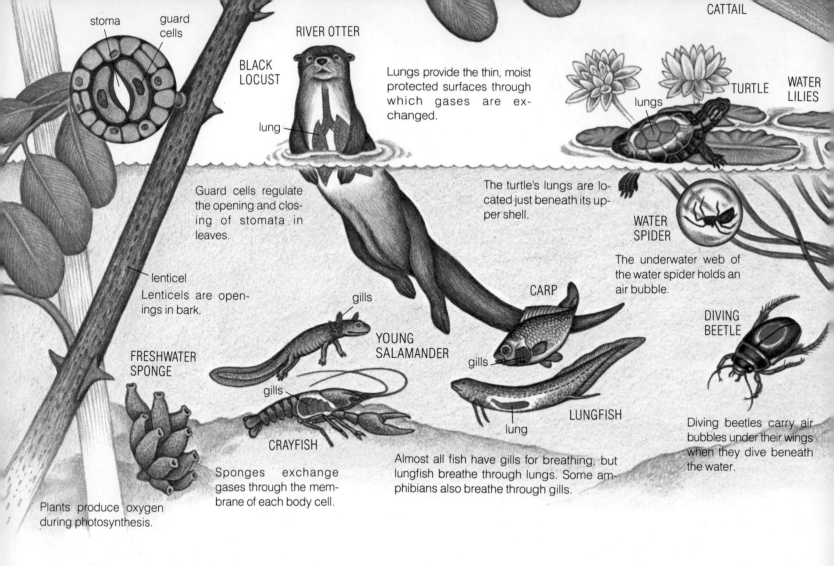

stoma / guard cells

RIVER OTTER

BLACK LOCUST

Lungs provide the thin, moist protected surfaces through which gases are exchanged.

lung

CATTAIL

TURTLE

WATER LILIES

lungs

Guard cells regulate the opening and closing of stomata in leaves.

The turtle's lungs are located just beneath its upper shell.

WATER SPIDER

lenticel
Lenticels are openings in bark.

The underwater web of the water spider holds an air bubble.

CARP

gills

DIVING BEETLE

FRESHWATER SPONGE

YOUNG SALAMANDER

gills

gills

LUNGFISH

lung

Diving beetles carry air bubbles under their wings when they dive beneath the water.

CRAYFISH

Sponges exchange gases through the membrane of each body cell.

Almost all fish have gills for breathing, but lungfish breathe through lungs. Some amphibians also breathe through gills.

Plants produce oxygen during photosynthesis.

Oxygen for Life

Animals eat food to get nutrients and energy. They digest food into glucose, amino acids, and simple fats, which all have energy stored in the chemical bonds holding them together. All cells constantly need energy to carry on their chemical activities. The easiest way for cells to get energy is to release it from glucose during the process of respiration.

Respiration is a series of chemical reactions that take place in plant and animal cells. During respiration energy is released when glucose is broken down into carbon dioxide and water. This energy is stored in molecules of ATP, to be used when and where it is needed.

In order to complete all of the chemical reactions in respiration, oxygen must be present in cells. Only a few single-celled organisms live without oxygen. They are found in places where other living things can't exist. The rest of life on Earth can't survive without oxygen.

Oxygen is a gas that is present in both air and water. The air animals breathe is 21 percent oxygen, 78 percent nitrogen, and 0.03 percent carbon dioxide, with traces of other gases. Water is not as good a source of oxygen as air because it contains only one-thirtieth the amount of oxygen that air does. Oxygen in both air and water is constantly resupplied by plants during photosynthesis.

Since plant and animal cells are unable to store oxygen, it must be continually available to them. Cells also have to get rid of the waste carbon dioxide

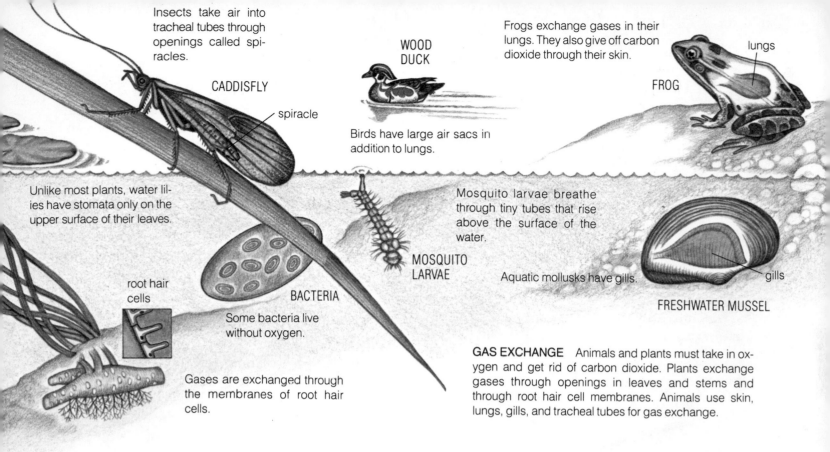

Insects take air into tracheal tubes through openings called spiracles.

CADDISFLY

spiracle

WOOD DUCK

Birds have large air sacs in addition to lungs.

Frogs exchange gases in their lungs. They also give off carbon dioxide through their skin.

lungs

FROG

Unlike most plants, water lilies have stomata only on the upper surface of their leaves.

root hair cells

BACTERIA

Some bacteria live without oxygen.

Gases are exchanged through the membranes of root hair cells.

Mosquito larvae breathe through tiny tubes that rise above the surface of the water.

MOSQUITO LARVAE

Aquatic mollusks have gills.

gills

FRESHWATER MUSSEL

GAS EXCHANGE   Animals and plants must take in oxygen and get rid of carbon dioxide. Plants exchange gases through openings in leaves and stems and through root hair cell membranes. Animals use skin, lungs, gills, and tracheal tubes for gas exchange.

produced during respiration. This carbon dioxide returns to the air and water as part of the carbon cycle.

Gas Exchange

Single-celled organisms and some simple animals, such as hydras, take in oxygen directly from the fluid in which they live. Oxygen passes through their cell membranes to get into cells, while carbon dioxide moves out of the cells and is eliminated.

More complicated plants and animals have special organs that take in oxygen and give off carbon dioxide. These organs include leaves, skin, gills, lungs, and tracheal tubes. Although animals like earthworms take in oxygen through their moist skin, the outer coverings of most other animals prevent gases from passing through to the inside.

For most animals, oxygen has to be carried from the site where it is taken in to all the other cells in the body. And carbon dioxide has to be picked up from each cell and transported back to a site where it can be given off.

The Need for Oxygen

Many animals are able to regulate the amount of oxygen they take in. Different animals have different needs. Birds need a great deal of oxygen when they fly. At high altitudes there is less oxygen available than there is near Earth's surface. Some migrating birds fly as far as 2,000 miles (3,200 kilometers) in three days without stopping. Since they use so much energy, they need great amounts of oxygen. Animals need more oxygen when they are active than when they are resting. At night, plants don't produce oxygen, so they must take some in for respiration. For roots to grow, oxygen must be present in the soil.

Under water it is more difficult for living things to get oxygen. Not only is there less oxygen available for plants and animals, but oxygen molecules also move more slowly in water than in air. Fish can use up 25 to 50 percent of all of their energy just providing themselves with oxygen.

The supply of oxygen must meet the demands of cells for oxygen. If the supply falls below a critical level, cells become damaged and die.

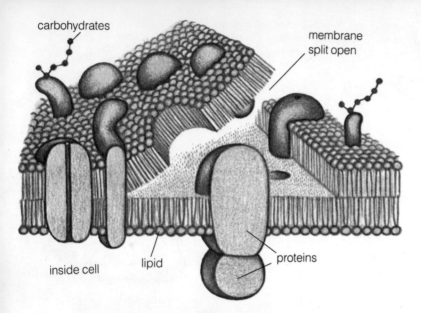

CELL MEMBRANES Membranes consist of proteins and fatty substances called lipids. Some proteins touch both the inside and the outside of the cell. Others are loosely attached to either the inside or the outside of the cell. Certain proteins can move within the membrane.

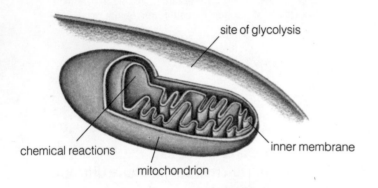

WHERE RESPIRATION TAKES PLACE The first part of respiration, called glycolysis, takes place in the cytoplasm of the cell. The rest of the process occurs in the mitochondria. Each mitochondrion has an outer membrane and a folded inner one.

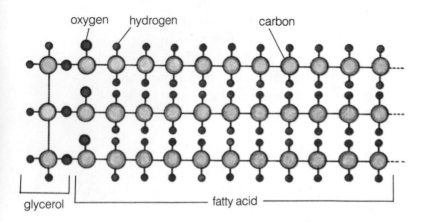

FATS Fats are made of glycerol and fatty acids. They can be large or small molecules, depending on how long the fatty acid chains are. Energy is stored in the bonds holding fat molecules together.

Membranes

Gas exchange takes place through cell membranes, because they are thin enough for oxygen and carbon dioxide to pass through easily. Since gases must dissolve in fluid before they can enter cells, membranes always have to be moist. They also have to be protected from drying out and being damaged.

In gases, such as carbon dioxide and oxygen, molecules move all of the time. The movement of molecules from one place to another is called diffusion. Gas molecules will diffuse in all directions until they are evenly spread out.

Respiration

Respiration is a series of chemical reactions that takes place in all cells. During respiration the bonds holding glucose molecules together are broken. The steps in respiration are shown on the opposite page. The first part of the process takes place in the cytoplasm of the cell and does not require oxygen. The rest of the process takes place in the mitochondria, where oxygen must be present.

By the end of respiration, each molecule of glucose has been broken down into carbon dioxide and water. Some of the energy contained in the glucose is used to make 36 ATP molecules. But about half of the energy is released as heat. This heat helps many animals keep their body temperature constant (page 41).

Glucose isn't the only nutrient from which cells can get energy. When glucose supplies are used up, cells break down starch and glycogen (page 47) into glucose. If still more energy is needed, cells break down fats.

Fats consist of carbon, hydrogen, and oxygen atoms bonded together. A lot of energy is stored in these bonds. Most fats have long chains of carbon atoms to which hydrogen atoms are attached. There is very little oxygen in fats. Fats make up part of cell membranes. They also serve as insulation and protection for cells. Cells store fats and use them when they need energy.

If animals are starving, the protein in their cells is broken down to get energy. When this happens, though, tissues are destroyed.

How Respiration Works

A glucose molecule
hydrogen
oxygen
carbon

2 ATP molecules made

2 pyruvic acid molecules

B
mitochondrion

Carbon dioxide given off.

C
2 molecules with two carbon atoms

D
ATP made
carbon dioxide
chemical reactions
ATP made
carbon dioxide
Energy-rich electrons carried to inner membrane.

inner membrane

E
32 ATP molecules made to run cell.

energy and heat

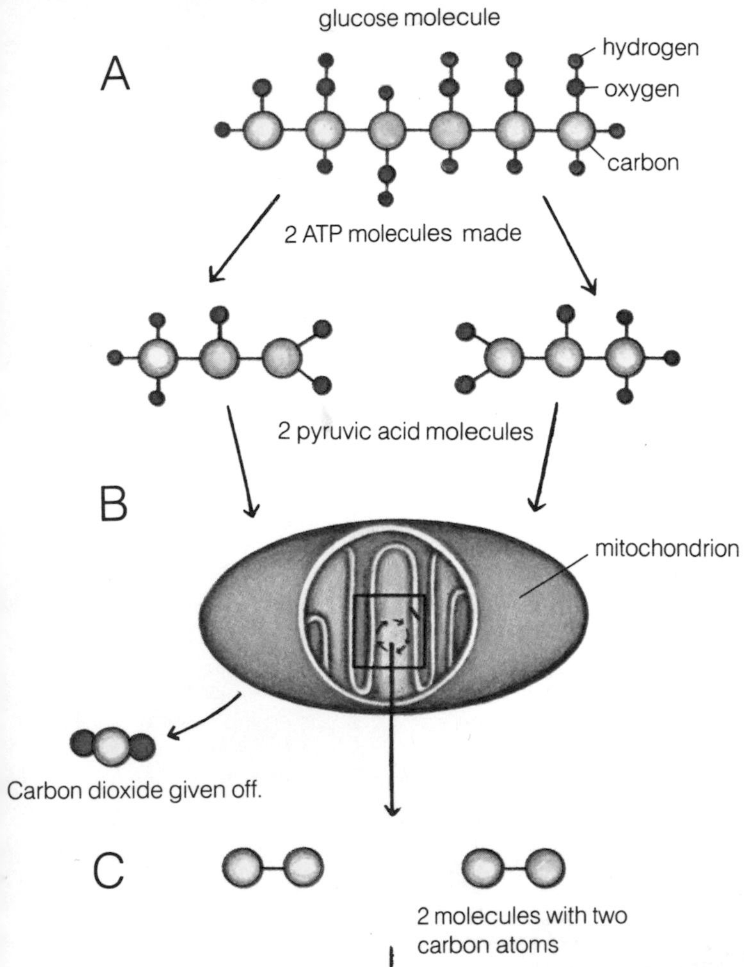

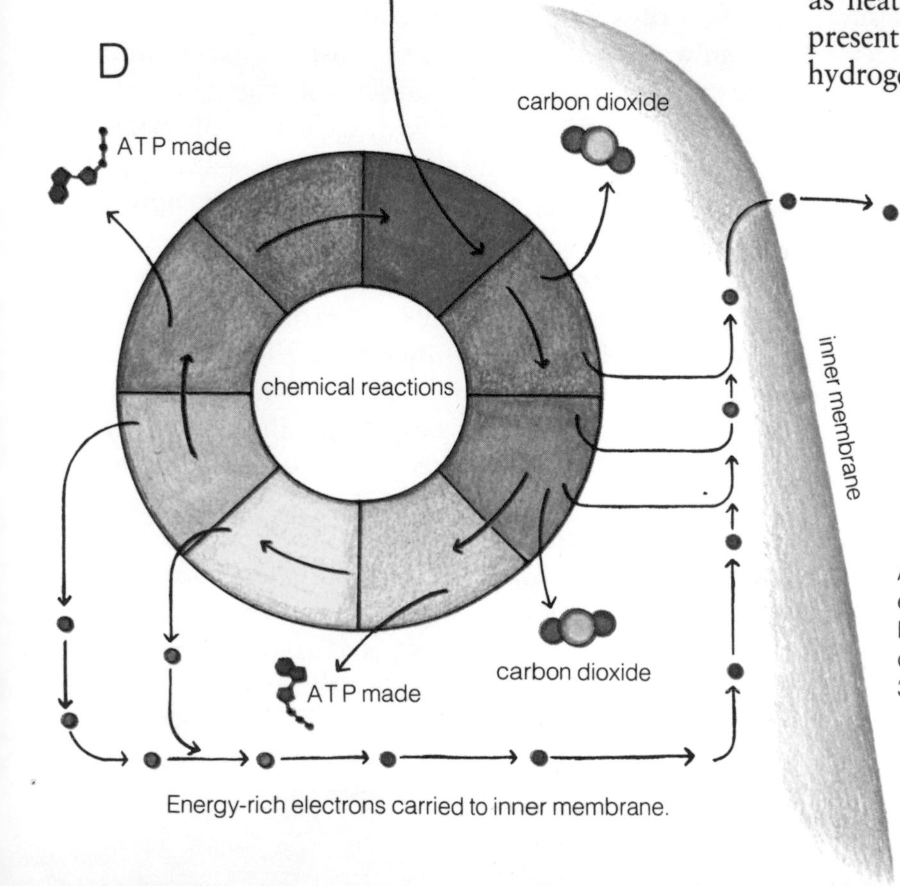

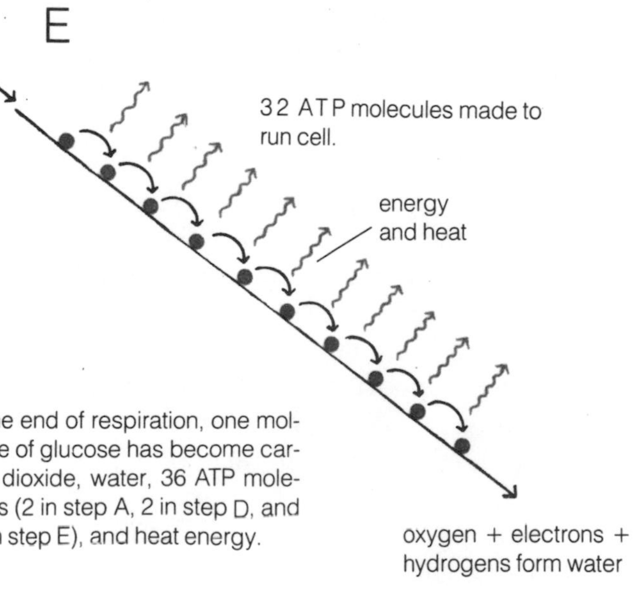

At the end of respiration, one molecule of glucose has become carbon dioxide, water, 36 ATP molecules (2 in step A, 2 in step D, and 32 in step E), and heat energy.

oxygen + electrons + hydrogens form water

R espiration is a series of chemical reactions. During respiration some of the energy in glucose molecules is used to make ATP. The rest is given off as heat. In the presence of oxygen, glucose is broken down into carbon dioxide, water, and energy.

The first part of respiration, called glycolysis, takes place in the cytoplasm. No oxygen is needed for glycolysis to take place. In a series of chemical steps glucose (A) is broken down into two molecules of pyruvic acid (B). Two ATP molecules are produced.

Each molecule of pyruvic acid enters a mitochondrion and is broken down further into a smaller molecule (C). Energy is released from this molecule during a series of chemical reactions called the Krebs cycle (D). This energy is transferred to electrons and carried to the inner membrane of the mitochondrion. During the Krebs cycle, carbon dioxide, hydrogen atoms, and two more ATP molecules are produced.

At the inner membrane of the mitochondrion, the energy-rich electrons are passed along a chain of molecules (E). Some of the energy in the electrons is used to make 32 more ATP molecules. The rest is given off as heat. At the end of the chain, oxygen must be present to accept pairs of electrons. Only then can hydrogen combine with oxygen to form water.

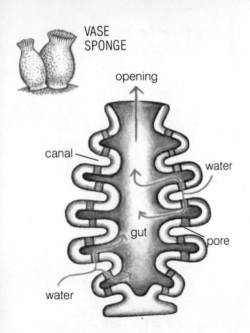

VASE SPONGE

opening

canal

water

gut

pore

water

OXYGEN FOR SPONGES In simple animals, such as sponges, water containing oxygen circulates through canals to all cells. Water flows in through pores and out through the large opening at the top of the sponge. Each cell takes in oxygen from the water and gets rid of carbon dioxide.

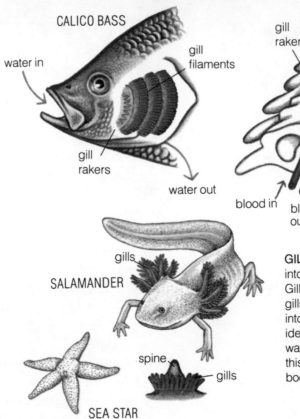

CALICO BASS

water in

gill filaments

gill rakers

water out

SALAMANDER

gills

spine

gills

SEA STAR

gill raker

water flow

gill filament

gill arch

blood in

blood out

capillaries

GILLS Fish breathe with gills. Water is taken into the mouth and passed over the gill surface. Gill rakers prevent food particles from clogging gills. In the gills, oxygen from the water moves into capillaries. At the same time, carbon dioxide carried by the blood moves out into the water. Some animals, like this salamander and this sea star, have gills on the outside of their bodies.

Oxygen In, Carbon Dioxide Out

In simple animals made up of only one or a few layers of cells, each cell takes in oxygen directly from the water in which the animal lives. When hydras take water into their digestive sacs, they expose the cells inside their body to the oxygen in the water. Sponges supply their cells with oxygen by passing water through a series of canals.

Gills

Fish use gills to take in oxygen and get rid of carbon dioxide. In adult fish the gills are inside of gill slits located on both sides of the head. Covering the outside of each gill slit is a protective fold. Gills consist of delicate fibers, or filaments, that extend out from a support arch. Gills are fragile; they would collapse and dry up out of water.

Fish take water into the mouth and into the pharynx, the muscular top portion of the throat. No water enters the food tube, because it stays collapsed except when fish are swallowing. From the pharynx,

the flow of water is directed over the gills. Some fish pump water over their gills by closing their mouths and pulling together the muscles in the pharynx. Fast-swimming fish swim with their mouths open, forcing water over their gills. Gill rakers prevent particles from clogging gills and help many fish capture food. Water leaves the gills by pushing open the protective outer cover.

As water flows over gills, oxygen in the water passes through the membranes in the gills and moves into capillaries. Capillary walls are only one cell thick, making it easy for gases to get through them. Oxygen is picked up by red blood cells inside the capillaries.

Blood flows through gills in one direction and water flows in the opposite direction. The blood entering the gills has already given off its oxygen to all the cells in the body of the fish. It needs more oxygen. Since water has more oxygen than this blood, oxygen moves into the capillaries. At the same time, the

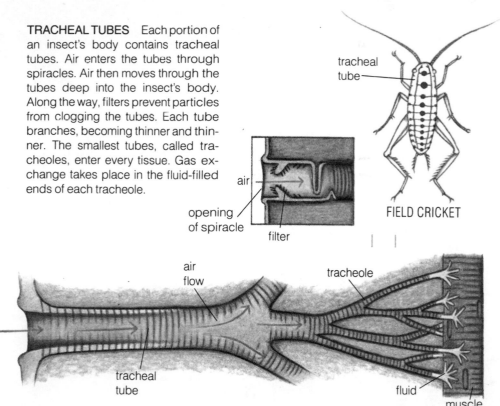

TRACHEAL TUBES Each portion of an insect's body contains tracheal tubes. Air enters the tubes through spiracles. Air then moves through the tubes deep into the insect's body. Along the way, filters prevent particles from clogging the tubes. Each tube branches, becoming thinner and thinner. The smallest tubes, called tracheoles, enter every tissue. Gas exchange takes place in the fluid-filled ends of each tracheole.

air
opening of spiracle
filter

tracheal tube
FIELD CRICKET

air flow
tracheal tube
tracheole
fluid
muscle

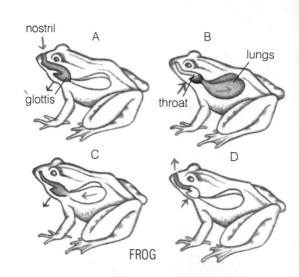

nostril   A   B
glottis   throat   lungs
C   D
FROG

FROG LUNGS Frogs force air into their lungs. When air is drawn into the nose (A), the glottis leading to the throat closes. Next (B) the nostrils close, the glottis opens, and air is pushed into the lungs. After gases are exchanged, air from the lungs goes back to the mouth (C). Finally (D) the glottis closes off the passage to the lungs, the nostrils open, and air carrying waste carbon dioxide is given off.

blood is carrying waste carbon dioxide picked up from cells. Since this blood has more carbon dioxide than the water does, carbon dioxide moves out of the gills and into the water.

Not all fish use gills. Some, such as electric eels, breathe through their mouths. Every few minutes they have to surface for air. Oxygen enters their bodies through membranes in their mouths, and carbon dioxide is given off through their skin.

Tracheal Tubes

Insects use a totally different system to exchange gases (oxygen in, carbon dioxide out). Each portion of their bodies has a pair of openings called spiracles. Air enters through these spiracles, which are opened and closed by valves. Each spiracle leads to tracheal tubes.

Tracheal tubes pass deep into the insect's body, branching and becoming thinner and thinner. They end up as tiny tubes called tracheoles. Every tissue in the body is penetrated by a tracheole. Tracheoles contain the membranes through which gases are exchanged. The ends of the tracheoles are filled with fluid that helps keep these membranes moist.

As cells need oxygen, it moves from the air in the tube, into the fluid, through the membranes, and into the cells. Carbon dioxide moves out in the opposite direction. Some carbon dioxide is also eliminated through the insect's skin. Large insects have muscles that help move air in and out of the tracheal tubes.

Some insects live in water. Diving beetles, for example, swim to the surface of the water and trap an air bubble under their wings. Under water, they breathe from this bubble. The only tracheal openings on their bodies that take in oxygen are those that touch the air bubble.

Lungs

Amphibians are animals that live both in the water and on land. Some have gills on the outside of their bodies. Others, such as frogs, have lungs. Frogs force air into their lungs. Most other animals suck air into their lungs with the help of muscles.

Land animals, such as gorillas, have two light, spongy, elastic bags called lungs, which are enclosed in an airtight covering. Lungs have no muscles, but they sit in the chest cavity surrounded by the rib cage, which does have muscles attached to it. Stretched

LUNGS The arrows trace the path of air as it moves from the nostrils to the tiny bronchioles in the lungs. At the end of each bronchiole are thin-walled air sacs, called alveoli, where gas exchange takes place. Blood reaches the alveoli carrying waste carbon dioxide. It leaves carrying a fresh supply of oxygen.

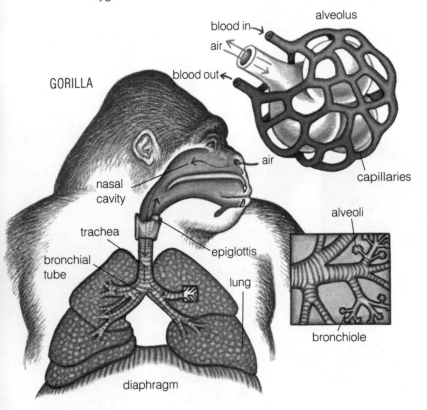

An alveolar air sac looks like a bunch of balloons. The walls of each sac are very thin and moist. Alveoli are surrounded by a rich supply of capillaries. Blood reaches the alveoli carrying waste carbon dioxide and leaves with a fresh supply of oxygen. Gas exchange takes place through the membranes inside the alveoli. When the diaphragm relaxes, air containing waste carbon dioxide is forced out of the lungs.

Active animals build up a lot of carbon dioxide in their blood. They have to breathe harder to get rid of it and to take in enough oxygen. Changes in the rate of breathing are controlled by the brain.

How Birds Breathe

Birds have a unique breathing system. In addition to lungs, birds have eight or nine special sacs. These sacs are large, and some of them lie in front of the

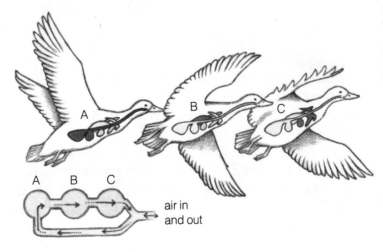

HOW BIRDS BREATHE In addition to lungs, birds have eight or nine special large sacs. When birds breathe in, air first goes to the rear sacs (A). Then it moves into the lungs (B), where gases are exchanged. From the lungs, this air goes into the front sacs (C) and is finally breathed out of the bird's body.

below the lungs is a sheet of muscle called the diaphragm.

The mechanical process of moving air in and out of the lungs is called breathing. When air is taken into the lungs, the diaphragm contracts downward and the ribs move up and out. This increases the size of the chest cavity so air can rush into the lungs.

Air is drawn into the nasal cavity, where it is moistened and warmed. It then moves into the windpipe, or trachea, which is held open by C-shaped rings made of cartilage (see page 53). A flap of tissue called the epiglottis closes off the trachea when food is being swallowed.

The trachea carries air down into the chest cavity. In the chest cavity, the trachea divides into two bronchial tubes that enter the lungs. In the lungs each bronchial tube divides into thinner and thinner air ducts. The thinnest air ducts, the bronchioles, end in tiny air sacs called alveoli. Your lungs have hundreds of thousands of bronchioles and millions of alveoli.

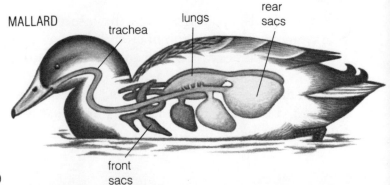

lungs, some behind. Air flows first into the rear sacs. Then it goes to the lungs, where gases are exchanged. From the lungs, the air flows into the front sacs and, finally, is breathed out of the bird's body. This arrangement lets birds take more oxygen out of the air than other animals do and helps them fly at altitudes where there is less oxygen available.

Gas Exchange in Plants

Respiration takes place in all living plant cells. During the day it takes place in mitochondria at the same time that photosynthesis takes place in chloroplasts. Plant cells use the glucose and oxygen produced during photosynthesis to carry out respiration. At night, when only respiration takes place, leaves have to take in oxygen and get rid of waste carbon dioxide.

Leaves are covered by a single layer of cells, called the epidermis. In many leaves, epidermal cells are coated with a waxy substance that prevents gases and water from entering or escaping.

Gases move in and out of leaves through tiny openings called the stomata. Each of these openings is surrounded by two guard cells, shaped like half-moons (page 24). Guard cells open and close stomata.

Leaves are divided into layers of cells. Beneath the upper surface of each leaf is the palisade layer, where most photosynthesis takes place. Below the palisade layer is the spongy layer, where air has room to circulate in the large interconnected air spaces between cells. Oxygen and carbon dioxide reach leaf cells by moving through these spaces. Water, brought to the leaves by veins, bathes each plant cell. Once carbon dioxide and oxygen dissolve in the film of water around each cell, they can diffuse in and out of cells.

The cells in plant stems also need oxygen. Stems have openings called lenticels, through which air flows in and out. In plants with woody stems, lenticels are found in the bark, the outer layer of the stem.

Underground, gases are exchanged across the moist membranes of root hair cells. Oxygen is taken in from the air that is trapped in the spaces between soil particles. When earthworms move through soil, they help mix air into it. If soil is too wet, air is forced out and roots die.

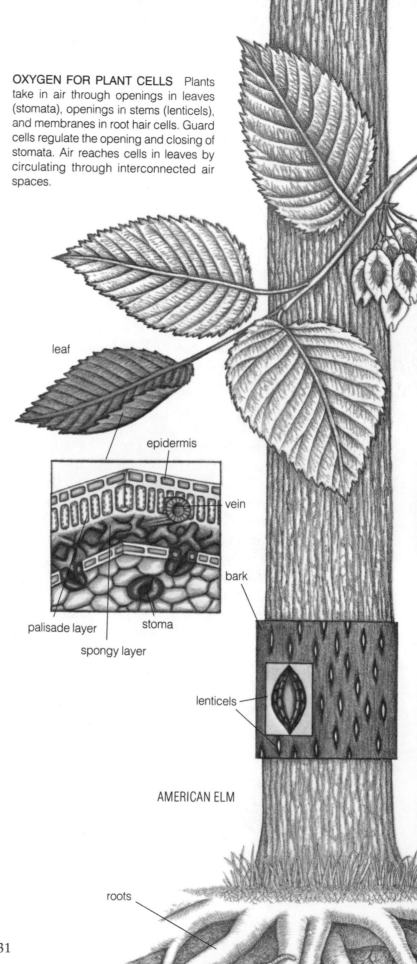

OXYGEN FOR PLANT CELLS Plants take in air through openings in leaves (stomata), openings in stems (lenticels), and membranes in root hair cells. Guard cells regulate the opening and closing of stomata. Air reaches cells in leaves by circulating through interconnected air spaces.

leaf

epidermis

vein

palisade layer

spongy layer

stoma

bark

lenticels

AMERICAN ELM

roots

31

Circulation

Giraffes are the tallest animals in the world. The head of a fully grown giraffe can stand 18 feet (5.5 meters) above the ground. Its neck can be more than 5 feet (1.6 meters) long. Like cows, giraffes eat plants, have a four-part stomach, and chew their cud. Nutrients from digested plants pass through the walls of their small intestine into capillaries. These nutrients have to be delivered to every cell in the body, including those high in the giraffe's head. All cells also need oxygen, which has to be carried to them from the capillaries in the lungs where it is picked up.

In animals, capillaries are part of the circulatory system. Along with veins and arteries, they make up a group of connected tubes, or blood vessels, which transport blood. Blood is pumped by the heart to all parts of the body.

Blood

Blood delivers nutrients and oxygen to cells. It also carries away cell wastes to the organs that dispose of them (page 42). Blood is composed of blood cells and a fluid called plasma. Plasma is 90 percent water and contains dissolved nutrients, vitamins, minerals, proteins, and wastes. Plasma also helps spread heat from one part of the body to another.

There are many kinds of cells in the blood. Red blood cells contain a protein called hemoglobin, which carries oxygen around the body. White blood cells help protect against infection.

The Heart

In many animals, such as giraffes and zebras, the heart has four muscular chambers. The upper chambers are called atria. The two lower chambers are the ventricles. A muscular wall separates the left side of the heart from the right side. Each side of the heart has one atrium and one ventricle.

Heart muscle is unique — it beats by itself. Even so, the heartbeat can be changed by signals from nerves. Some nerves speed up the beat, others slow it down. Certain chemicals also change the rate at which the heart beats.

Heartbeats start at a spot in the right atrium, called the pacemaker. The pacemaker sends out signals that spread from the upper chambers of the heart to the lower chambers. These signals cause heart muscle fibers to pull together, or contract. When heart muscles contract, blood is forced out of the heart. In between each contraction, heart muscles relax, allowing blood to enter the upper chambers of the heart. Blood is always entering or leaving the heart.

Blood Vessels

Blood travels through three types of blood vessels: arteries, capillaries, and veins. Arteries, which carry blood away from the heart, have thick elastic walls. The largest artery, the aorta, is connected to the heart.

Arteries deliver blood to capillaries, the tiniest blood vessels. Capillary walls are only one cell thick, making it easy for nutrients, oxygen, and wastes to pass through them.

Capillaries deliver blood to veins, and veins transport blood back to the heart. Veins have thinner, less muscular walls than arteries do. The largest vein, the vena cava, is also connected to the heart.

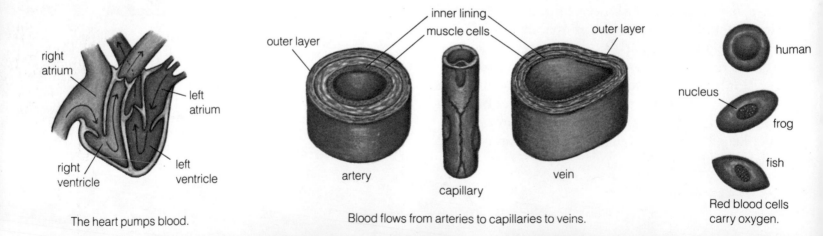

right atrium   left atrium   right ventricle   left ventricle

The heart pumps blood.

outer layer   inner lining   muscle cells   outer layer   artery   capillary   vein

Blood flows from arteries to capillaries to veins.

human   nucleus   frog   fish

Red blood cells carry oxygen.

The heart pumps blood into large arteries, which then branch into smaller and smaller arteries before connecting up with capillaries.

On its way back to the heart, blood leaves capillaries and flows into small veins. These veins branch into larger veins until the vena cava empties blood into the heart.

Circulation of the Blood

Blood carrying waste carbon dioxide enters the right atrium of the heart and flows into the right ventricle. A one-way valve prevents the blood from flowing backward. Every time the heart contracts, blood is forced out of the right ventricle and into the artery that carries it to the lungs.

In the capillaries of the lungs, oxygen is picked up by the blood and carbon dioxide is released. Oxygen-rich blood leaves the lungs in veins that transport it back to the left atrium of the heart.

The oxygen-rich blood then flows from the left atrium into the left ventricle. When the heart contracts, this blood is forced out of the heart and into the aorta. Large arteries branch from the aorta and carry blood to every part of the body.

When blood reaches the capillaries, nutrients and oxygen move through the capillary walls to the cells that need them. Before blood leaves the capillaries, it picks up wastes given off from cells.

From the capillaries, blood flows into small veins, which gradually become larger and larger. Finally, oxygen-poor blood, loaded with wastes, empties into the vena cava, the vein that takes it back to the right atrium.

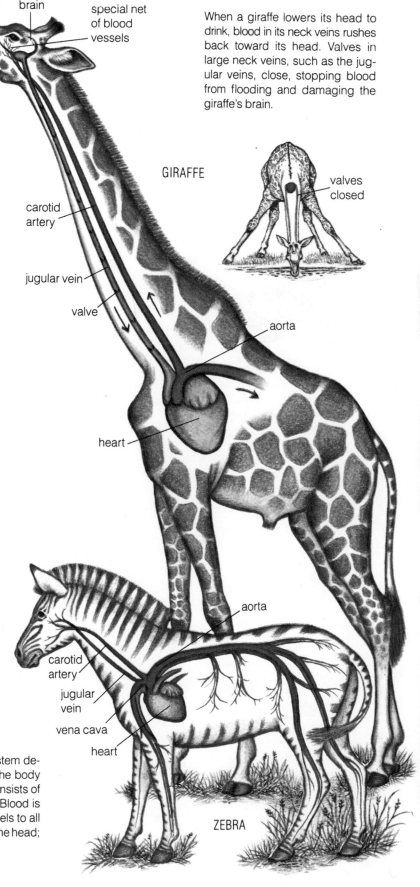

When a giraffe lowers its head to drink, blood in its neck veins rushes back toward its head. Valves in large neck veins, such as the jugular veins, close, stopping blood from flooding and damaging the giraffe's brain.

brain

special net of blood vessels

GIRAFFE

valves closed

carotid artery

jugular vein

valve

aorta

heart

aorta

carotid artery

jugular vein

vena cava

heart

ZEBRA

veins

Valves prevent blood from flowing backward.

BLOOD CIRCULATION The circulatory system delivers nutrients and oxygen to every part of the body and picks up wastes produced by cells. It consists of the heart, the blood vessels, and the blood. Blood is pumped by the heart through the blood vessels to all cells. The carotid arteries, for example, go to the head; the renal arteries, to the kidneys.

33

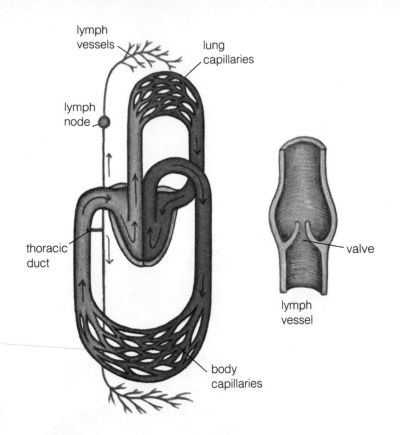

TRANSPORT SYSTEMS The heart is really two pumps. The right side pumps blood to the lungs to get rid of waste carbon dioxide and pick up fresh oxygen. The left side of the heart pumps oxygen-rich blood to all parts of the body. The lymph system returns fluids to the main circulation through the thoracic duct. Lymph vessels, like veins, have one-way valves.

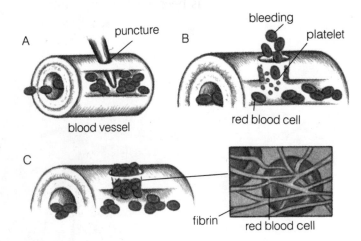

BLOOD CLOTTING When blood vessels are damaged (A), blood cells bleed into tissues. Tiny blood platelets gather at the site of the wound (B) and give off an enzyme that helps sticky threads of fibrin develop. These sticky threads (C) form a web that traps blood cells and platelets. As the web hardens into a clot, bleeding stops and the wound starts to heal.

The heart has its own supply of blood vessels. Coronary arteries bring oxygen and nutrients to heart cells, and coronary veins transport wastes away from heart cells. If the blood vessels supplying the heart are damaged or blocked, the heart may stop working.

Red Blood Cells

Red blood cells carry oxygen. Each cell is formed in the red bone marrow (see page 52) and lives only a few months. Even though the liver and spleen destroy millions of old red blood cells, new red blood cells immediately replace them. Red blood cells contain millions of molecules of a protein called hemoglobin. Every hemoglobin molecule can carry four oxygen molecules, making oxygen-rich blood appear bright red. When hemoglobin releases oxygen to body cells that need it, blood turns dark red.

Blood Pressure

The heart pumps blood under pressure into arteries. This blood pressure is the force created when the left ventricle contracts, and the pressure has to be strong enough to deliver blood to all parts of the body.

Blood pressure is kept up by the muscular walls of the arteries. These walls expand when blood is forced into them. When the walls spring back, they help push the blood along. This continuous expansion and bouncing back of arteries is what you feel when you take your pulse.

As blood moves away from the heart, blood pressure decreases. By the time the blood reaches the veins, there is little pressure left. In addition, the walls of the veins aren't muscular enough to create pressure. Body muscles that press against veins help to push blood back to the heart. Many veins also have valves to prevent blood from flowing backward.

A giraffe's heart pumps blood at a much higher pressure than is found in other animals. This extra pressure is strong enough to push blood up its long neck arteries and into its head. But high blood pressure is dangerous, because it can cause small blood vessels to burst. A special net of blood vessels at the bottom of the giraffe's brain reduces the high blood pressure, so no damage is done.

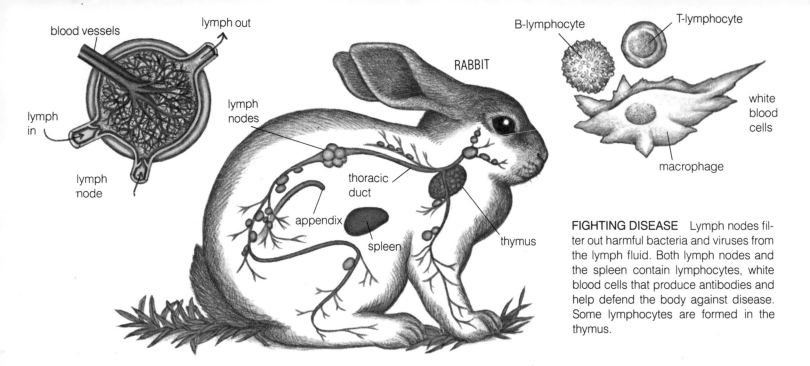

blood vessels

lymph out

lymph in

lymph node

lymph nodes

thoracic duct

appendix

spleen

thymus

RABBIT

B-lymphocyte

T-lymphocyte

white blood cells

macrophage

FIGHTING DISEASE Lymph nodes filter out harmful bacteria and viruses from the lymph fluid. Both lymph nodes and the spleen contain lymphocytes, white blood cells that produce antibodies and help defend the body against disease. Some lymphocytes are formed in the thymus.

The Lymph System

Capillary walls are so thin that fluid and some small proteins leak out of the blood vessels into the spaces between cells. This fluid, which is mostly water, bathes all of the cells of the body. If capillaries kept losing fluid, there would be none left in the blood vessels. While some of this fluid returns to the veins, the rest is returned to the circulatory system by lymph vessels. Inside of lymph vessels, the fluid is called lymph.

Because lymph vessels have very thin walls, it is easy for fluids and proteins to move into them. But bacteria, viruses, and cancer cells also have no difficulty getting into lymph vessels. So throughout the lymph system are lymph nodes, which filter the lymph fluid and trap harmful viruses and cells.

Whenever an animal is injured, it runs the risk of infection caused by bacteria and viruses that invade its open wounds. Wounds begin to plug up immediately as clots form in damaged blood vessels (see illustration on opposite page). At the wound site, clean-up cells, called macrophages, surround, take in, and break apart dirt particles, pieces of damaged cells, and any bacteria they come across.

As you know, it takes time for a wound to heal. During that time, though, bacteria may have invaded your bloodstream and circulated throughout your body. If these bacteria are not killed, they might multiply and infect or even destroy your tissues.

Your main defense against infection is provided by your lymphocytes, which are white blood cells. There are two main groups of lymphocytes, T-cells and B-cells. T-cells are lymphocytes that develop in the thymus, and B-cells are formed in the bone marrow.

On the surface of different bacteria and viruses are proteins that identify them, just as fingerprints identify different people. Your lymphocytes are constantly watching out for these proteins, for they are a signal that your body has been invaded by bacteria or viruses that don't belong there. As soon as these invaders are recognized, T-cells help B-cells to develop into special cells that produce antibodies.

Antibodies are proteins that attach like handcuffs to bacteria or viruses and make them harmless. With antibodies attached to them, bacteria and viruses are easily identified and destroyed by clean-up macrophages and by special cells in your liver and spleen. Your body can produce hundreds of thousands of different kinds of antibodies. Each kind of antibody knows exactly what it is looking for. If you have the mumps, for instance, you make antibodies that go after mumps viruses in your body. These antibodies are useless against measles viruses. But if you come down with the measles, you make different antibodies that only go after measles viruses. Antibodies keep circulating around your body in blood and lymph until they find every harmful invader. Antibodies and lymphocytes provide you with resistance, or immunity, to diseases.

Circulatory Systems

The circulatory system delivers materials to every part of an animal's body and picks up wastes. In each diagram the arrows indicate the path the blood takes as it circulates through each animal.

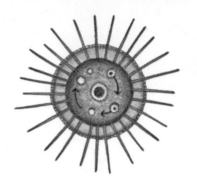

STREAMING In single-celled organisms, nutrients and gases are spread around by the streaming movement of the cytoplasm.

SINGLE-CELLED HELIOZOAN

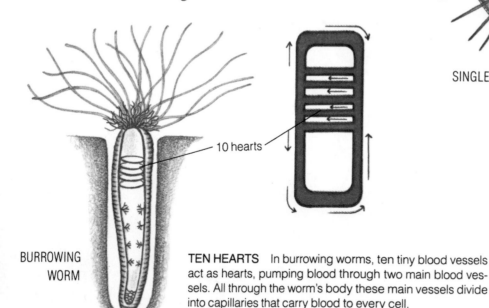

10 hearts

BURROWING WORM

TEN HEARTS In burrowing worms, ten tiny blood vessels act as hearts, pumping blood through two main blood vessels. All through the worm's body these main vessels divide into capillaries that carry blood to every cell.

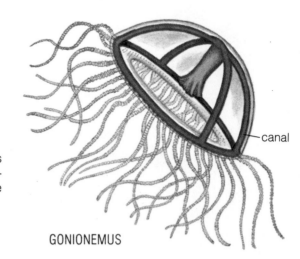

canal

GONIONEMUS

shell

lung

heart

sinus

LAND SNAIL

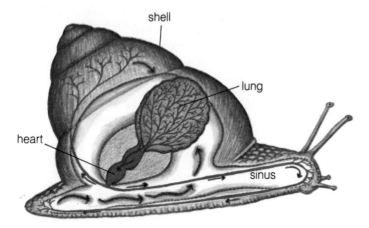

CANALS Jellyfish take in water containing food and oxygen and carry it through canals to all the cells in their body. Hairlike cilia line the canals, helping to create currents that push materials along. When water leaves the jellyfish, it carries away carbon dioxide and other wastes.

blood vessel

sinus

CABBAGE BUTTERFLY

sinus

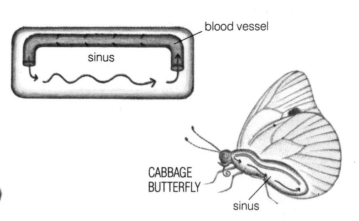

SHRIMP

heart

sinus

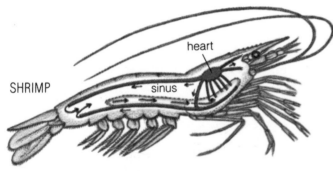

OPEN SYSTEMS In land snails (above left), shrimp (left), and insects (above), blood flows from vessels into large open spaces between organs, called sinuses. Blood slowly moves through these spaces until it returns to the heart. In land snails blood picks up oxygen in the lungs, and in shrimp oxygen is picked up from the gills. In insects blood does not carry oxygen to cells because it is supplied through the tracheal tubes.

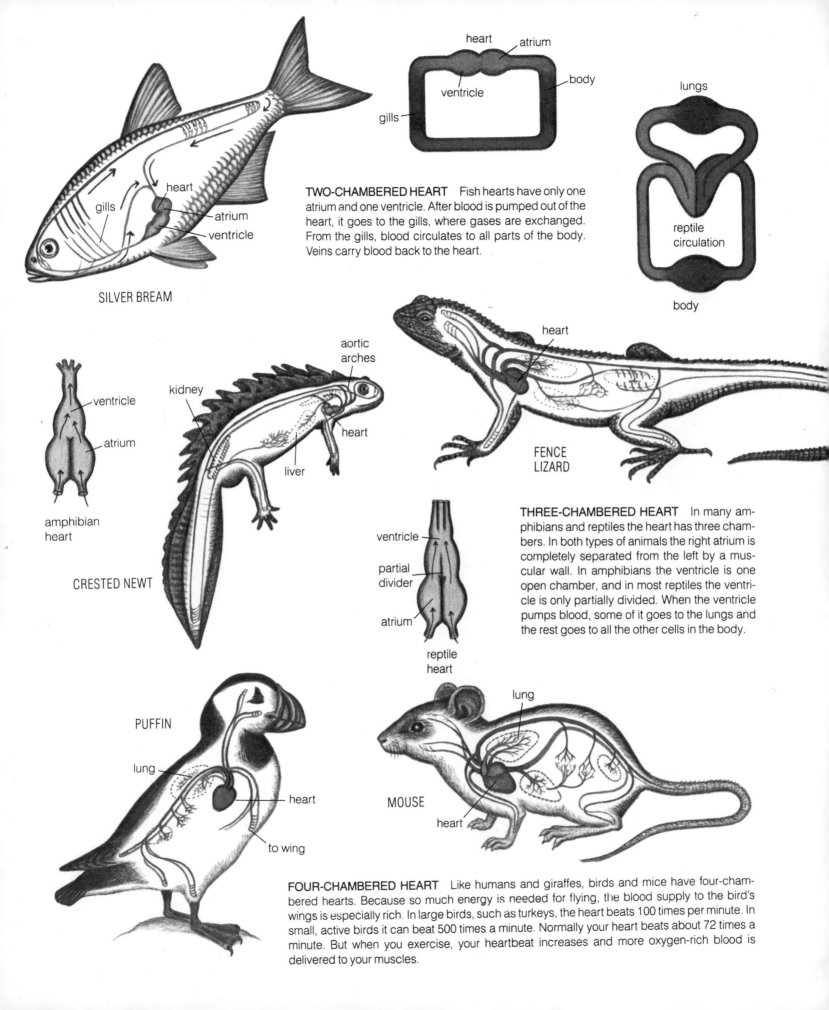

TWO-CHAMBERED HEART Fish hearts have only one atrium and one ventricle. After blood is pumped out of the heart, it goes to the gills, where gases are exchanged. From the gills, blood circulates to all parts of the body. Veins carry blood back to the heart.

SILVER BREAM

heart
atrium
ventricle
body
gills

lungs
reptile circulation
body

gills
heart
atrium
ventricle

ventricle
atrium
amphibian heart

CRESTED NEWT

kidney
aortic arches
heart
liver

heart
FENCE LIZARD

ventricle
partial divider
atrium
reptile heart

THREE-CHAMBERED HEART In many amphibians and reptiles the heart has three chambers. In both types of animals the right atrium is completely separated from the left by a muscular wall. In amphibians the ventricle is one open chamber, and in most reptiles the ventricle is only partially divided. When the ventricle pumps blood, some of it goes to the lungs and the rest goes to all the other cells in the body.

PUFFIN
lung
heart
to wing

lung
MOUSE
heart

FOUR-CHAMBERED HEART Like humans and giraffes, birds and mice have four-chambered hearts. Because so much energy is needed for flying, the blood supply to the bird's wings is especially rich. In large birds, such as turkeys, the heart beats 100 times per minute. In small, active birds it can beat 500 times a minute. Normally your heart beats about 72 times a minute. But when you exercise, your heartbeat increases and more oxygen-rich blood is delivered to your muscles.

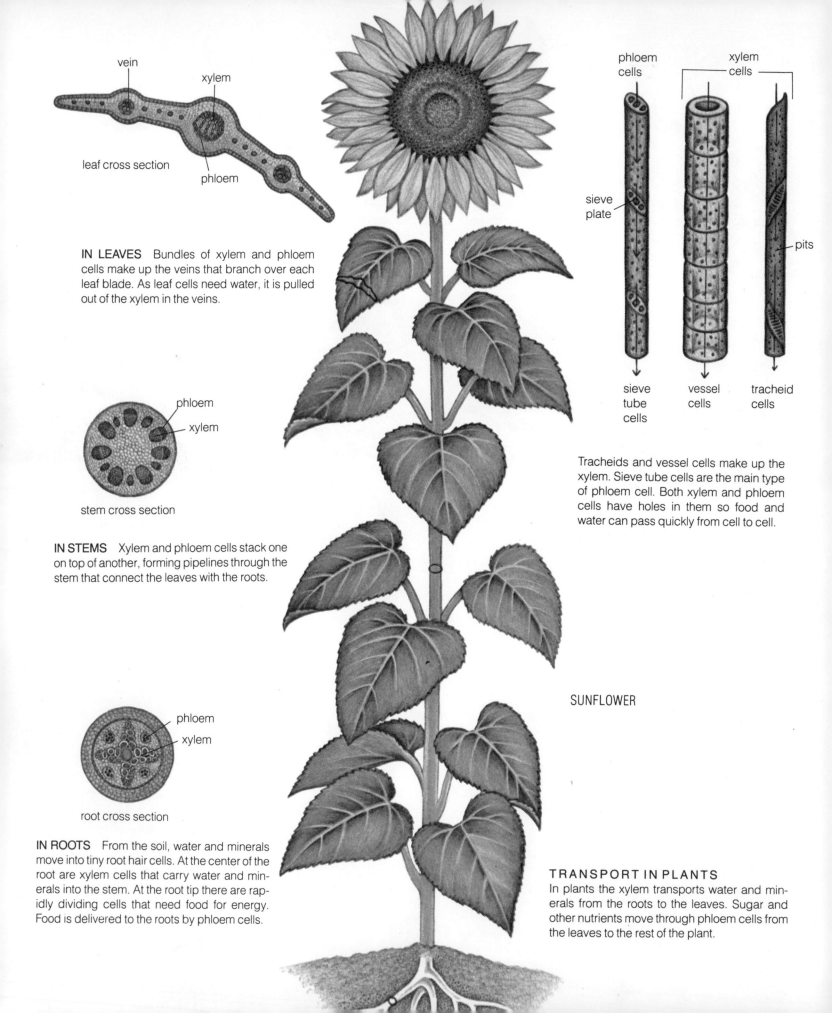

vein

xylem

leaf cross section

phloem

IN LEAVES Bundles of xylem and phloem cells make up the veins that branch over each leaf blade. As leaf cells need water, it is pulled out of the xylem in the veins.

phloem

xylem

stem cross section

IN STEMS Xylem and phloem cells stack one on top of another, forming pipelines through the stem that connect the leaves with the roots.

phloem

xylem

root cross section

IN ROOTS From the soil, water and minerals move into tiny root hair cells. At the center of the root are xylem cells that carry water and minerals into the stem. At the root tip there are rapidly dividing cells that need food for energy. Food is delivered to the roots by phloem cells.

phloem cells

xylem cells

sieve plate

pits

sieve tube cells

vessel cells

tracheid cells

Tracheids and vessel cells make up the xylem. Sieve tube cells are the main type of phloem cell. Both xylem and phloem cells have holes in them so food and water can pass quickly from cell to cell.

SUNFLOWER

TRANSPORT IN PLANTS
In plants the xylem transports water and minerals from the roots to the leaves. Sugar and other nutrients move through phloem cells from the leaves to the rest of the plant.

Pipelines in Plants

Plants have two systems, called xylem and phloem, for carrying water and nutrients. In both systems cells are stacked one on top of another, forming pipelines that run throughout the plant. Xylem cells transport water and minerals from the roots to the stem and leaves. Phloem cells transport food from the leaves to the rest of the plant.

Circulation of Water and Minerals

Two kinds of cells make up the xylem. Tracheids are long cells, pointed at each end. Vessel cells are shorter and wider than tracheid cells. As both kinds of xylem cells grow, their cell walls thicken. Then they die and all that remains of them are their thick cell walls, which form a continuous pipeline through the plant. Holes form in sections of these cell walls, allowing minerals and water to pass from one xylem cell to another.

Leaf cells use some water during photosynthesis. But more than 95 percent of the water taken in by plant roots evaporates through the stomata. This constant water loss, called transpiration, creates a suction force that helps lift more water.

Food Transport

Sugar and other nutrients produced in leaves are carried by phloem cells to the rest of the plant. The main type of phloem cell is the sieve tube cell. Stacked end to end, these long, narrow, thin-walled cells form sieve tubes throughout the plant stem. Food passes from cell to cell through tiny holes in special areas called sieve plates. In contrast to xylem cells, phloem cells are alive.

Xylem and Phloem in Trees

Many plants live for only one growing season, but some trees live for thousands of years. Each year a growing tree will produce new xylem and phloem cells. Both develop from a layer of cells, called the vascular cambium, lying between the xylem and phloem. New xylem cells grow toward the center of the tree, and phloem cells grow out toward the bark.

Both xylem and phloem cells grow in rings. Every spring new xylem cells develop, and by the end of summer they have grown large. Xylem cells that develop late in the season don't have much time to grow because when winter comes all growth stops. During the next growing season new rings of large and small xylem cells form. If you count the xylem rings in the trunk of a tree, you can estimate the age of that tree. Since phloem cells never grow large and thick, they are difficult to count.

Almost the entire trunk of a tree is dead xylem cells, or wood. In very old trees the rings of xylem cells nearest the center of the tree become plugged with gummy substances. This is called heartwood. Xylem cells that continue to transport water and minerals are called sapwood.

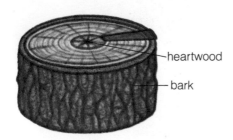

heartwood

bark

YEARLY GROWTH Each year that a tree grows, new rings of xylem and phloem cells are produced. You can tell a lot from the rings in a tree's trunk. By counting the rings of dead xylem cells, you can estimate a tree's age. Thick rings mean good growing seasons, and thin rings mean that growth was poor.

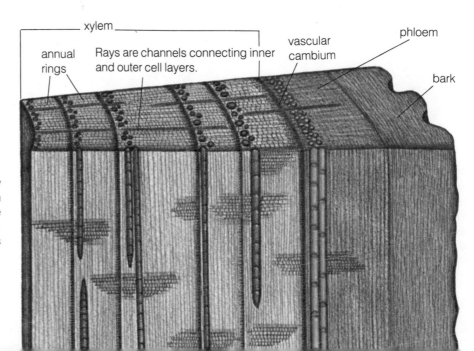

xylem

annual rings

Rays are channels connecting inner and outer cell layers.

vascular cambium

phloem

bark

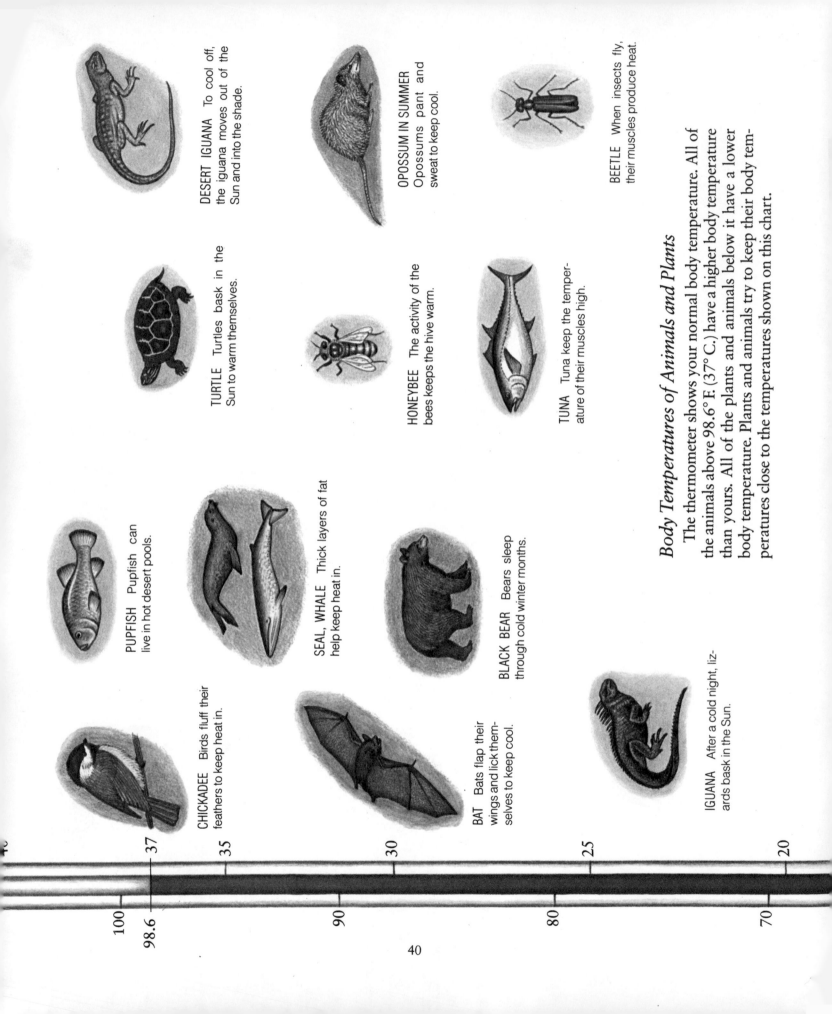

DESERT IGUANA To cool off, the iguana moves out of the Sun and into the shade.

OPOSSUM IN SUMMER Opossums pant and sweat to keep cool.

BEETLE When insects fly, their muscles produce heat.

TURTLE Turtles bask in the Sun to warm themselves.

HONEYBEE The activity of the bees keeps the hive warm.

TUNA Tuna keep the temperature of their muscles high.

PUPFISH Pupfish can live in hot desert pools.

SEAL, WHALE Thick layers of fat help keep heat in.

BLACK BEAR Bears sleep through cold winter months.

CHICKADEE Birds fluff their feathers to keep heat in.

BAT Bats flap their wings and lick themselves to keep cool.

IGUANA After a cold night, lizards bask in the Sun.

Body Temperatures of Animals and Plants

The thermometer shows your normal body temperature. All of the animals above 98.6° F. (37° C.) have a higher body temperature than yours. All of the plants and animals below it have a lower body temperature. Plants and animals try to keep their body temperatures close to the temperatures shown on this chart.

37

35

30

25

20

100

98.6

90

80

70

Collecting tubes take the urine to the center of each kidney. There a large tube, called the ureter, leaves each kidney and carries urine to the bladder. In the bladder, urine is stored until it is released through the urethra, a tube opening to the body surface.

Uric Acid

Animals that produce urine are always losing some water from their bodies. Birds, insects, reptiles, and land snails convert their nitrogen wastes into uric acid instead of urea. Since uric acid is a solid, these animals don't lose water when they get rid of their nitrogen wastes.

Balancing Salt and Water

Water makes up more than two-thirds of the weight of most animals. It is found in cells, in between cells, and in the liquid part of blood. The fluid inside and outside of cells takes part in the many chemical reactions carried out by living things. Salts and minerals are dissolved in this fluid.

Animal cells need salts and minerals inside them as well as in the fluid that bathes them. The amount of salt and water in body fluids has to be carefully regulated. If there is too much salt inside cells, water will flow into the cells to balance out the amount of salt. This extra water can cause cells to burst. If there is too much salt outside cells, water may flow out of cells. When too much water is lost by cells, they shrink. Kidneys help regulate salt levels by getting rid of the excess amounts the body can't use.

WATER LOSS Animals take in water when they eat and drink, but they constantly lose it in their solid and liquid wastes and in their sweat. Water is always lost in the urine, a fluid given off from the kidneys. This water loss rids the body of harmful nitrogen wastes. There are hundreds of thousands of tiny urine-producing tubes, called nephrons, in each kidney.

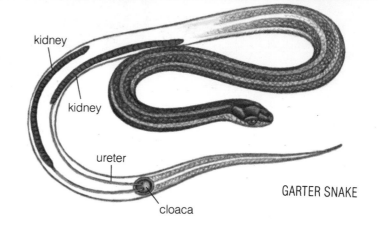

GARTER SNAKE

SOLID NITROGEN WASTES Reptiles, such as this garter snake, convert their nitrogen wastes into uric acid. Since uric acid is a solid, no water is lost when it is eliminated. Uric acid is given off from the cloaca, a chamber that also receives digestive wastes and material from the reproductive system.

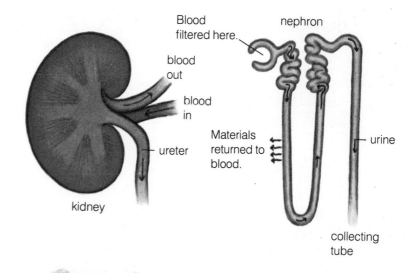

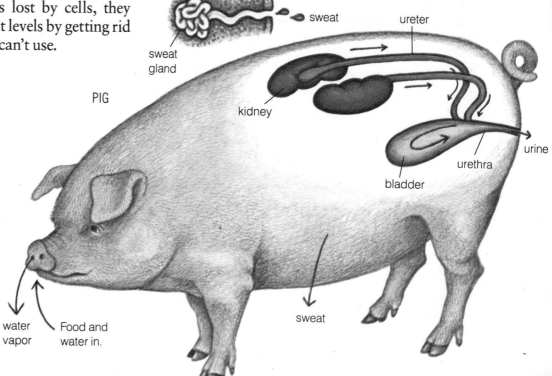

PIG

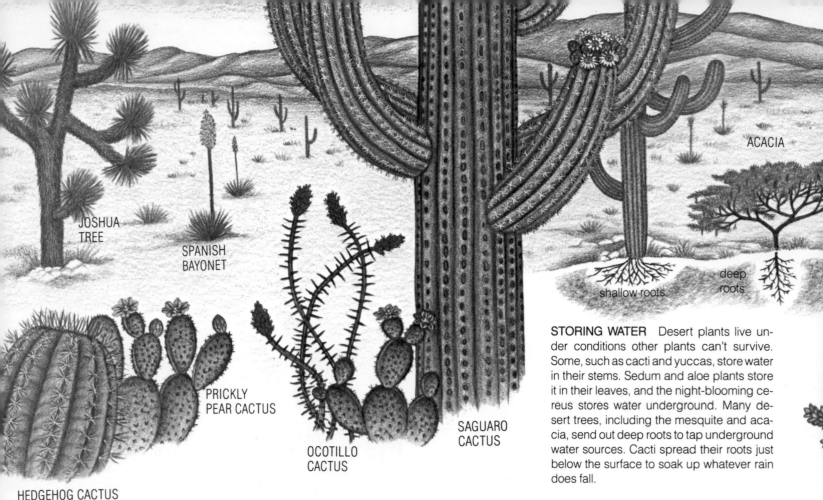

JOSHUA TREE

SPANISH BAYONET

PRICKLY PEAR CACTUS

OCOTILLO CACTUS

SAGUARO CACTUS

HEDGEHOG CACTUS

ACACIA

shallow roots

deep roots

STORING WATER Desert plants live under conditions other plants can't survive. Some, such as cacti and yuccas, store water in their stems. Sedum and aloe plants store it in their leaves, and the night-blooming cereus stores water underground. Many desert trees, including the mesquite and acacia, send out deep roots to tap underground water sources. Cacti spread their roots just below the surface to soak up whatever rain does fall.

Many fish and sea birds take in salty seawater. Saltwater fish have cells in their gills that help them get rid of all this salt. And sea gulls, pelicans, penguins, and albatrosses have special glands near their eyes that give off excess salt. This salty fluid drains through a tube and out through the nostrils.

Sweat Glands

Animals with sweat glands lose both salt and water when they perspire. Sweat glands are usually located in the dermis, the thick lower region of the skin. Each sweat gland has a coiled part that leads to a tube. This tube passes through the epidermis (the upper region of the skin) and then opens onto the body surface.

In the dermis, capillaries run near the coiled part of each sweat gland. As blood flows through the capillaries, water and salt are absorbed into the sweat gland. This salty liquid fills the tube until it reaches the skin as sweat.

When sweat evaporates from skin, it has a cooling effect. In active animals, blood vessels beneath the skin grow wider, bringing more blood near the surface. By giving off heat and sweating more, animals cool down.

Replacing Lost Water

Whenever animals get rid of their wastes, they lose water from their bodies. Although most water is lost in urine and sweat, some water evaporates when gases are exchanged in the lungs. Some water is also given off as part of solid digestive wastes.

Plants, too, are always losing water. Almost all of the water taken in by plants through their roots is lost to the air through the stomata.

Plants and animals have to replace the water that they lose. Plant roots continually grow, pushing through the soil toward water. When the air is dry, plants lose water faster. During these times the guard cells surrounding the stomata close, preventing further water loss.

Most animals live where they can find enough water. They drink water and eat foods containing water. Many animals produce dry nitrogen wastes

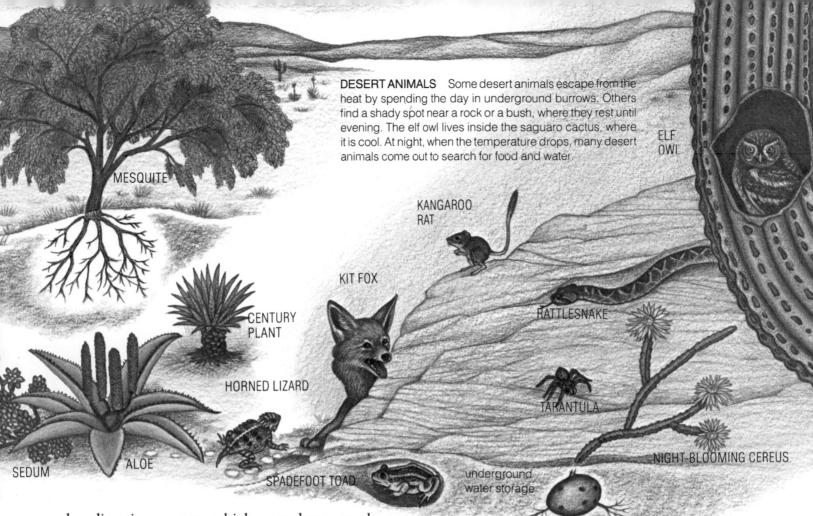

DESERT ANIMALS Some desert animals escape from the heat by spending the day in underground burrows. Others find a shady spot near a rock or a bush, where they rest until evening. The elf owl lives inside the saguaro cactus, where it is cool. At night, when the temperature drops, many desert animals come out to search for food and water.

MESQUITE

ELF OWL

KANGAROO RAT

KIT FOX

CENTURY PLANT

RATTLESNAKE

HORNED LIZARD

TARANTULA

SEDUM

ALOE

SPADEFOOT TOAD

underground water storage

NIGHT-BLOOMING CEREUS

or dry digestive wastes, which cuts down on the amount of water these animals lose every day.

Water in Short Supply

There are some areas on Earth, such as the deserts, where water is very hard to find. Desert plants and animals have different ways of living under hot, dry conditions. Many desert plants have roots that lie just below the surface and are able to soak up whatever rain does fall. Other plants have very deep roots that tap underground sources of water.

Cactus plants store water in their stems. Instead of leaves, cacti have protective spines that reduce water loss and keep away thirsty animals. Since they don't have leaves, cacti use the stomata on their stems to take in the carbon dioxide they need to carry on photosynthesis. Some cacti open their stomata only at night when there is moisture in the air. These plants take in carbon dioxide and store it until the next day, when they use it for photosynthesis.

Desert plants like the yucca have special tissues in their fleshy leaves that store water. Despite the dry

conditions, many desert shrubs do have leaves. But during very dry spells these plants lose so much water through their leaves that all the leaves die. Only after it rains can these shrubs produce more leaves.

Like desert plants, desert animals also have to conserve water. Many animals live in underground burrows during the hot day and come out only during the cooler night. Other animals rest during the day in shady spots near rocks and bushes. The elf owl spends its days inside the saguaro cactus, where it is much cooler than it is outside.

Some animals have to get most of their water from the food they eat. Even though kangaroo rats hardly ever drink, they survive on the small amount of water produced in each of their cells during respiration (page 27). These rats don't have sweat glands, and their solid wastes contain little if any water.

Balancing salt and water is only one activity that living things must control. Many other activities are also controlled — some by special chemicals called hormones, others by muscles and nerves.

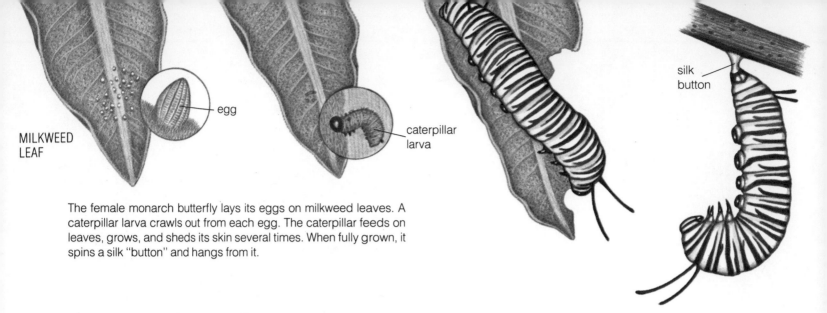

MILKWEED
LEAF

egg

caterpillar
larva

silk
button

The female monarch butterfly lays its eggs on milkweed leaves. A caterpillar larva crawls out from each egg. The caterpillar feeds on leaves, grows, and sheds its skin several times. When fully grown, it spins a silk "button" and hangs from it.

Chemical Controllers

You have already changed a great deal since you were a baby. Most animals change in size and shape as they grow and become adults. Many of these changes are controlled by chemicals called hormones. Hormones carry chemical instructions from one part of an animal's body to another.

Hormones are produced by groups of cells in glands. Some glands have tubes to carry away the chemicals they produce. Other glands have no tubes. They give off hormones directly into the bloodstream that travel to cells in different parts of the body. When hormones reach their destination, they cause changes to take place. Some of the most amazing changes hormones can cause are those that occur when caterpillars become butterflies.

Molting

Monarch butterflies lay their eggs on the leaves of the milkweed plant. When each egg hatches, a tiny wormlike larva, called a caterpillar, crawls out. It is hungry and eats its own shell. Caterpillars have mouth parts for chewing leaves and other plant parts. They eat a lot and begin to grow.

Caterpillars are covered by a hard outer skin that can stretch only so far. When they grow quickly, this skin becomes too small for their bodies. The skin has to be shed from time to time so that a new, larger outer covering can form. This process of shedding is called molting.

Molting is controlled by hormones produced in three pairs of glands. Two of these pairs are connected to the caterpillar's brain. The third pair is located behind the insect's head. Each pair produces a different hormone. One makes brain hormone, one makes juvenile hormone, and one makes molting hormone.

When all three of these hormones are produced, the growing caterpillar keeps shedding its skin. But as long as juvenile hormone continues to be made, the caterpillar is prevented from becoming a butterfly.

From Caterpillar to Butterfly

After the final molt, the juvenile hormone stops being produced. Then an incredible transformation controlled by the molting hormone occurs. The fully grown caterpillar spins a "button" made of silk that attaches to a plant. It grasps the button and hangs from it as its skin splits apart. Beneath its skin is a case called the chrysalis. The caterpillar does not eat or move inside this case. Now it is called a pupa.

During the pupal stage the tissues of the caterpillar are broken down and reused as raw materials to make new tissues and organs. The wings, legs, antennae, and body of a butterfly are formed from the cells of the caterpillar.

The newly created monarch butterfly appears folded up inside the now transparent chrysalis. When it hatches out of its case, it must wait until blood

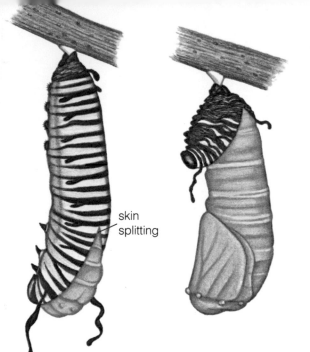

skin
splitting

chrysalis

METAMORPHOSIS As it hangs from its silk button, the caterpillar's skin splits and falls off. Beneath its skin is a case called a chrysalis, in which the caterpillar doesn't eat or move. During this pupal stage the caterpillar's tissues are broken down and reused to make the body of a butterfly. All of the changes that take place from egg to caterpillar to butterfly are called metamorphosis. These changes are caused by control chemicals called hormones.

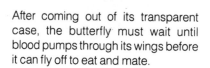

pumps through its collapsed wings. Then the butterfly can fly off to drink nectar from flowers for food. It no longer eats leaves, as it did when it was a caterpillar. The monarch will find a mate and the cycle will begin again. The complete change in appearance from egg to larva to pupa to adult butterfly is called metamorphosis. Tadpoles also undergo metamorphosis when they turn into frogs (see page 81).

After coming out of its transparent case, the butterfly must wait until blood pumps through its wings before it can fly off to eat and mate.

Animal Hormones

Many different hormones are produced by animals. These important chemicals control and help coordinate the activities of cells in almost every organ of the body. Only very small amounts of hormones are needed to get their job done.

A hormone called insulin controls the level of sugar in your blood. It is produced in the pancreas by groups of cells called the islets of Langerhans. Insulin is a protein made up of two chains linked together.

After each meal, digested sugar enters the bloodstream from the small intestine. As the glucose level in the blood rises, the islet cells in the pancreas produce insulin, which is given off into the blood and carried throughout the body.

Insulin causes most cells to take in sugar more easily and use it for energy. It particularly affects the liver and muscle cells by making them change glucose into glycogen. In animal cells, glycogen is the storage form of glucose.

MONARCH
BUTTERFLY

47

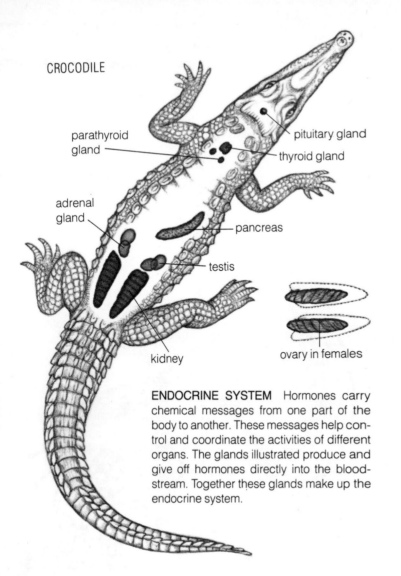

CROCODILE

parathyroid gland

pituitary gland

thyroid gland

adrenal gland

pancreas

testis

kidney

ovary in females

ENDOCRINE SYSTEM Hormones carry chemical messages from one part of the body to another. These messages help control and coordinate the activities of different organs. The glands illustrated produce and give off hormones directly into the bloodstream. Together these glands make up the endocrine system.

By causing cells to take in sugar from the blood and store it, insulin controls how much sugar is left in the blood. When the proper level is reached, the islet cells stop making insulin. Like most hormones, insulin breaks down rapidly after it has performed its job.

Many glands produce more than one hormone. The pituitary gland, located in your brain, produces so many hormones that it is often called the master gland. These hormones cause changes in many different organs. Some of the effects of the hormones given off by the pituitary gland are listed at the bottom of this page.

Plant Hormones

Plants produce five major groups of hormones. These chemicals control the bending of growing plants toward light and the growth of cells in leaves, stems, and roots. They also cause fruits to ripen, flowers to develop, and leaves to fall in autumn. Hormones can prevent seeds from starting to grow before conditions are right.

There are no glands in plants. Instead, plant hormones are produced by growing cells in roots, stems, and leaves. Some plant hormones travel through the stem to get from one part of the plant to another. Other hormones work only in the cells that produce them.

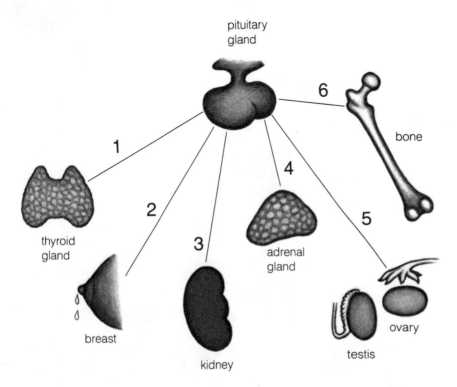

pituitary gland

1

2

3

4

5

6

bone

thyroid gland

breast

kidney

adrenal gland

testis

ovary

THE MASTER GLAND Because it gives off so many different hormones, the pituitary gland is often called the master gland. Some pituitary hormones travel to other glands and cause them to make their own hormones. The rest go directly to the cells that need them. This illustration shows six glands that receive hormones from the pituitary gland. Here is what each hormone does:

1. Causes thyroid gland to make thyroid hormone.
2. Causes mammary glands to produce milk.
3. Regulates amount of water kept by the kidneys.
4. Causes adrenal glands to produce many hormones.
5. Causes reproductive organs to develop and make hormones.
6. Controls bone and body growth.

BLACK
TUPELO

branch

dying
cells

lcaf
stem

WHY LEAVES FALL IN AUTUMN In autumn a layer
of cells at the base of each leaf stem gives off enzymes
that break down and weaken cell walls. A number of
hormones, including abscisic acid, help this process
take place. Cells in this layer start to separate, die,
and harden. By the time the leaf finally falls, the plant
has already sealed off its wound, preventing water
loss and infection.

PLANT HORMONES

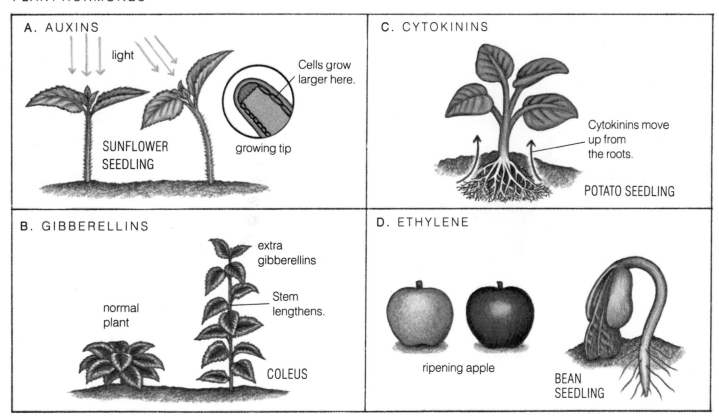

A. AUXINS

light

Cells grow
larger here.

SUNFLOWER
SEEDLING

growing tip

B. GIBBERELLINS

extra
gibberellins

Stem
lengthens.

normal
plant

COLEUS

C. CYTOKININS

Cytokinins move
up from
the roots.

POTATO SEEDLING

D. ETHYLENE

ripening apple

BEAN
SEEDLING

A — Auxins are hormones that help plant cells to grow larger. When
the Sun hits one side of a growing plant, the auxin supply on that
side drops and cells there grow slower. Cells on the other side,
though, keep growing normally. As they get larger they cause the
stem to bend.

B — Gibberellins cause plant stems to grow rapidly. They also help
developing plants use the food stored in their seeds.

C — Cytokinins help coordinate the growth of roots and stems. They
are produced in root cells and travel up through the xylem into the
growing stem.

D — Ethylene gas given off by plant cells causes fruits to ripen and
helps certain seeds begin to grow.

MUSCLE AND BONE The horse's skeleton supports and protects its delicate tissues and organs. The bones forming the horse's rib cage protect the heart and lungs. Those in the backbone protect nerves traveling to and from the brain.

Two bones come together at a joint. In the skull, bones grow so tightly together that no movement is possible at most joints. Other joints in the horse's body are movable. When muscles attached to bones contract, they pull on bones, which causes the bones to move from one position to another. When horses run, jump, or walk, they use many muscles at the same time.

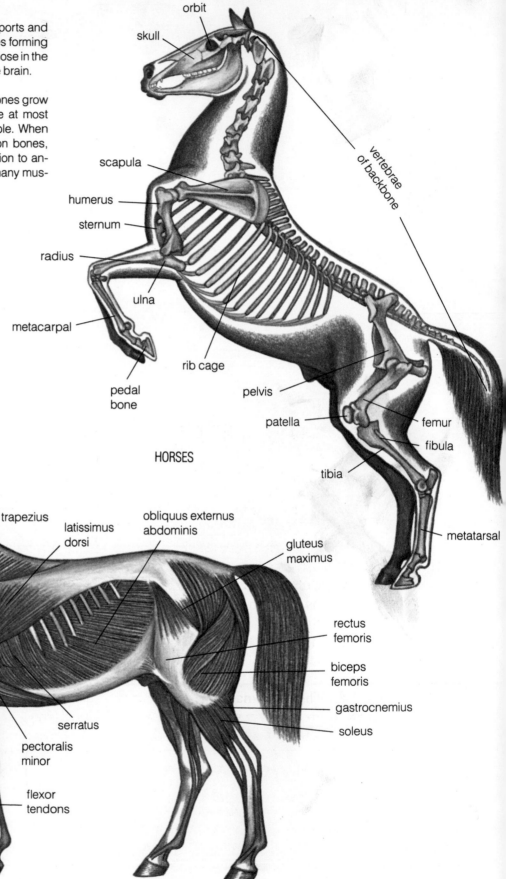

orbit
skull
scapula
humerus
sternum
radius
ulna
metacarpal
rib cage
pedal bone
pelvis
patella
femur
fibula
tibia
metatarsal
vertebrae of backbone

HORSES

temporalis
splenius
trapezius
latissimus dorsi
obliquus externus abdominis
gluteus maximus
brachiocephalicus
sternocleidomastoideus
spinodeltoideus
pectoralis
triceps
biceps
serratus
pectoralis minor
rectus femoris
biceps femoris
gastrocnemius
soleus
flexor carpi radialis
extensor digitorum muscles
flexor tendons

50

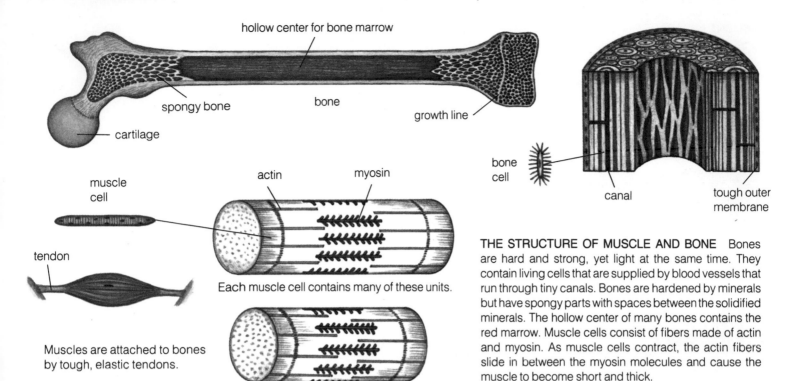

hollow center for bone marrow

spongy bone

bone

growth line

cartilage

bone cell

canal

tough outer membrane

muscle cell

actin

myosin

tendon

Each muscle cell contains many of these units.

Muscles are attached to bones by tough, elastic tendons.

contracted

THE STRUCTURE OF MUSCLE AND BONE Bones are hard and strong, yet light at the same time. They contain living cells that are supplied by blood vessels that run through tiny canals. Bones are hardened by minerals but have spongy parts with spaces between the solidified minerals. The hollow center of many bones contains the red marrow. Muscle cells consist of fibers made of actin and myosin. As muscle cells contract, the actin fibers slide in between the myosin molecules and cause the muscle to become short and thick.

Muscle, Skin, and Bone

Plants and animals have to support and protect their soft tissues and organs. In plants, stems support both flowers and leaves. Most animals support and protect their organs with a framework called a skeleton, which can be either inside or outside the body. One type of skeleton consists of fluid that fills the spaces between the organs inside animals such as hydras and earthworms. By pushing against the body walls, this fluid helps these animals keep their shape.

Another type of skeleton is a hard outer covering, such as a shell. A shell is made of proteins and chemicals, such as calcium carbonate, produced by the animal living inside. There are many different kinds of shells. Snail shells are spiral in shape, the nautilus shell has chambers inside it, and clams live inside two shells.

The outer covering of insects is a skeleton made of proteins and a carbohydrate called chitin. This covering forms the tough, flexible skin that insects shed when they molt. Many insect skeletons contain wax that prevents the loss of water from the insect's body.

A third type of skeleton, made up of cartilage and bone, is like the one inside your body.

Bones

Bones are strong and hard, yet also light. They have different sizes and shapes, depending upon what they do. Some bones, such as those in the rib cage, protect the heart and lungs. Others are used mainly for movement. The backbone, which is made up of many small bones called vertebrae, helps support the weight of an animal. Animals with backbones are called vertebrates.

Bones consist of hard minerals such as calcium and phosphorus. These minerals are molded into the shape of bones by bone cells. Some areas of a bone are tightly packed with minerals; in other areas there are spaces between the hard minerals. These spongy bone areas help keep bones light.

Blood vessels and nerves are contained in tiny canals that run through bones. These blood vessels supply bone cells with nutrients and oxygen. They also deliver growth hormones to bones.

In addition to taking away wastes from bone cells, blood vessels sometimes pick up calcium, phosphorus, and other minerals stored in bones. These min-

MOVEMENT AND MORE MOVEMENT

Most animals move from place to place to find food, water, a mate, or to escape from danger. Using their muscles, animals fly, swim, hop, run, crawl, and walk. Movement of any kind uses up the energy stored in ATP molecules (page 13).

LEECH

The leech loops along by contracting its muscles.

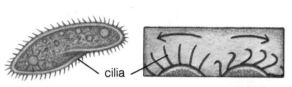

PARAMECIUM

cilia

Paramecia swim by beating the cilia on their cell surface back and forth.

CANADA GOOSE

Using their powerful flight muscles, birds flap their wings up and down. When their wings flap down, stiff, light feathers push air down and back, driving the bird up and forward. When birds pull up their wings, the feathers spread apart so air can move through them. To give their muscles a rest, birds often glide on air currents with their wings spread out.

Some hummingbirds are only 2 inches (5 centimeters) long. They can hover in the air while they feed.

Kangaroos use their long, powerful hind legs to leap as far as 25 feet (7.6 meters). When it leaps high in the air, a kangaroo uses its thick tail for balance.

HUMMINGBIRD

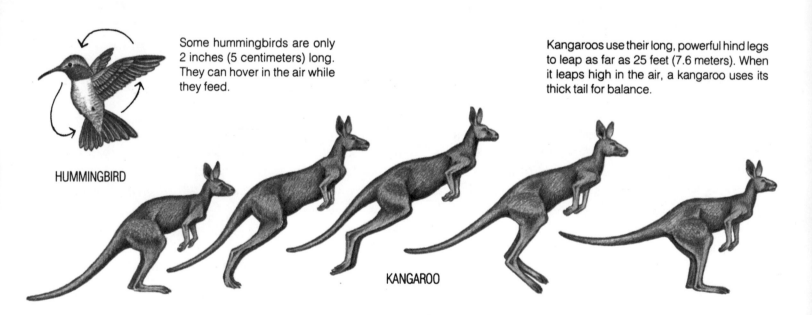

KANGAROO

erals are carried to parts of the body where they are needed.

At the center of many bones lies the marrow cavity. Red and white blood cells are produced in red marrow. Fats are stored in yellow marrow.

Joints

When two bones meet, they form a joint. Some bones, such as those in the skull, grow so tightly together that no movement is possible where they meet. But there are movable joints between other bones, such as those in the knee. Different kinds of joints make a variety of movement possible.

At a joint, tough ligament tissues stretch between bones to hold them together. A fluid-filled sac in between the ligaments reduces the friction where two bones rub against each other and helps keep the bone surfaces smooth.

Skin

Animals with skeletons inside their bodies are covered by skin, which is tough, elastic, and waterproof. Skin is made up of many layers of cells. The outer layers of cells, the epidermis, grow toward the skin surface, where they die and fall off. Beneath the epidermis, in the dermis, there are hair roots, sweat glands, nerves, and blood vessels.

Muscles and Movement

Since bones can't move by themselves, they have to be moved by the muscles attached to them. Muscles are made up of bundles of cells that can contract.

Muscle cells consist of fibers. In each fiber there are thin bands of a protein called actin and thick bands of a protein called myosin. The thick myosin bands have tiny bridges that almost touch the actin molecules.

When muscles receive a signal from nerve cells to contract, the tiny bridges attach to the actin molecules, pull on them, and cause them to slide in between the myosin bands. When this happens, muscle cells become short and thick. Each pulling stroke uses up energy that comes from ATP molecules.

There are three main kinds of muscle — smooth muscle, heart muscle, and skeletal muscle. Smooth muscles are found in the walls of blood vessels (page 32). They are also the muscles that control the movements of organs such as the stomach and bladder. An animal cannot willingly control its smooth muscles or heart muscle.

Muscles that connect to bones are called skeletal muscles. These muscles are attached to bones by tough, elastic tissues called tendons.

Animals can control their skeletal muscles. When skeletal muscles contract, they pull on bones, causing joints to bend. This bending moves bones from one position to another.

Walking, running, swimming, jumping, and flying are complicated movements that involve many muscles working at the same time. Each of these muscles has to receive a precise signal that tells it when to contract and when to relax. These signals come from the cells in the nervous system.

By contracting fibers in the bell-shaped part of its body, a jellyfish squeezes water out and propels itself upward.

Without any legs, a snake silently moves along the ground by forming loops that travel the length of its body. These loops press against rocks, grass, and sticks and push the snake along.

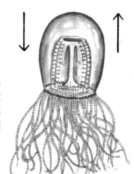

JELLYFISH

SNAKE

Some animals, such as barnacles, do not move.

BARNACLE

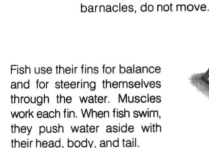

Fish use their fins for balance and for steering themselves through the water. Muscles work each fin. When fish swim, they push water aside with their head, body, and tail.

SHARK

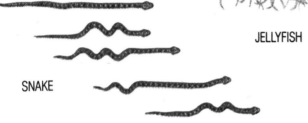

Cartilage

Cartilage is a smooth, firm tissue that is more flexible than bone, but not as hard. It forms the skeleton of some animals, such as sharks. Before you were born, your skeleton was made up of cartilage, but as you developed it was gradually replaced by bone. Some cartilage still remains in your nose, outer ear, and at the ends of your bones.

Electrical Signals

Animals control their movements with electrical signals that travel to their muscles and make the muscles contract. These signals are carried by nerve cells, called neurons, which are part of the nervous system.

The nervous system collects information from inside and outside an animal's body. After sorting out this information, the nervous system sends instructions to most of the organs in an animal's body. These instructions help control breathing, heart rate, body temperature, and the process of digestion. They also help animals find food, protect themselves, and respond to what is happening around them.

Nervous Systems

Some animals, such as those pictured below, have simple nervous systems. Hydras have the simplest type of nervous system. It consists of a net of nerve cells that runs throughout the body. Flatworms, such as planaria, have more complicated nervous systems. In addition to a nerve net, they have two major nerves or cords running the length of their bodies. And in their heads are bunches of nerves, called ganglia, that make up a simple brain.

Animals with backbones have very complicated nervous systems. Their brains are complex, and spinal cord nerves run through their backbones. The brain and the spinal cord make up the central nervous system.

From the central nervous system, bundles of nerve cells branch out to all parts of an animal's body. These nerves make up the peripheral nervous system and carry electrical signals to and from the spinal cord and brain.

Nerve Cells

Nerve cells transmit electrical signals. At one end of a nerve cell there are short fibers, or dendrites, which pick up electrical signals. Some nerve cells have more than a thousand of these fibers.

Dendrites carry electrical signals to the body of the nerve cell, where the nucleus and cell organelles are

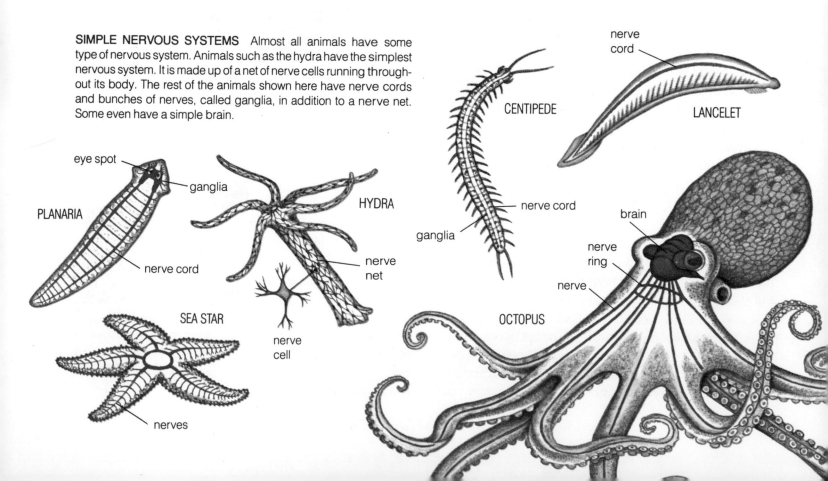

SIMPLE NERVOUS SYSTEMS Almost all animals have some type of nervous system. Animals such as the hydra have the simplest nervous system. It is made up of a net of nerve cells running throughout its body. The rest of the animals shown here have nerve cords and bunches of nerves, called ganglia, in addition to a nerve net. Some even have a simple brain.

eye spot
ganglia
PLANARIA
nerve cord
SEA STAR
nerves
HYDRA
nerve net
nerve cell

nerve cord
CENTIPEDE
LANCELET
nerve cord
ganglia

brain
nerve ring
nerve
OCTOPUS

located. From the cell body, the signal continues along a fiber called the axon.

Most axons are surrounded by a white, fatty substance called myelin. Myelin is given off by Schwann cells, which wrap around the axon. Myelin insulates and protects axons. Along the length of each axon are sections that have no myelin. These points are called the nodes of Ranvier. They make the axon look like a string of sausages. Electrical signals jump from one node to the next, moving as fast as 300 feet (100 meters) per second. At the end of the axon are branched terminal fibers that send off the signals to other nerve cells.

Synapses

Nerve cells do not usually touch each other. Instead, there are tiny gaps in between cells, called synapses. Electrical signals must cross these synapses to get from one nerve cell to the next.

Special chemicals, manufactured at the terminal ends of the axons, pick up the signals as they arrive. Then the chemicals are given off into the gap. Like boats carrying passengers, the chemical molecules travel across the gap. When the chemicals touch the dendrites of another nerve cell, the electrical impulses are let off. In this way, one nerve cell is able to pass an electrical signal to another. The chemicals that carried the signals are immediately destroyed so that they can't block the arrival of other impulses.

Some axons end up next to muscle cells. Their terminal ends branch over the muscle cells at places called end plates (see illustration).

Special chemicals also carry electrical signals from the nerve cell to the muscle cell. These signals cause the muscle cell to contract. When the signal stops, the muscle cell relaxes.

The Spinal Cord

The spinal cord receives information from many parts of the body. Nerves that carry information to the spinal cord are called sensory nerves. Most of the information the spinal cord receives is sent on to the brain through the nerves that make up the cord.

Nerves in the spinal cord also receive instructions from the brain and send them out to the parts of the body they should go to. These signals are carried out

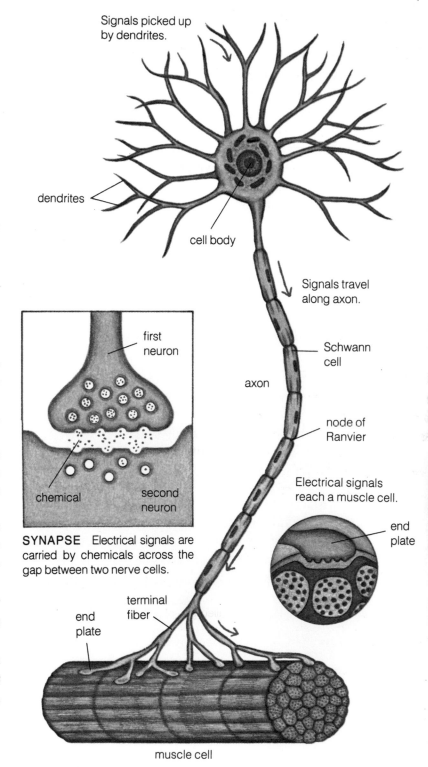

SYNAPSE Electrical signals are carried by chemicals across the gap between two nerve cells.

NERVE CELLS Nerve cells, or neurons, carry electrical signals. Short fibers called dendrites pick up these signals and carry them to the cell body. From there the signals travel along a fiber called an axon. Most axons are surrounded by fatty protective myelin. At the end of the axon are more branched fibers that send off the signals to other nerve cells or to muscle cells.

of the spinal cord by motor nerves. Some signals go to muscles; others are sent to glands, causing the glands to give off hormones.

The spinal cord also controls simple, automatic responses, called reflexes. Automatically pulling away from a hot object is an example of a reflex.

The Brain

The most important part of the central nervous system is the brain. It controls and coordinates activities in all parts of the body. The brain receives information from inside and outside of the body. Some of this information travels to the brain along the nerves in the spinal cord. The rest is brought to the brain directly by the cranial or brain nerves. For example, the nerve that carries information from the eyes to the brain is one of the cranial nerves. In the brain, information is picked up and sorted out by millions of interconnecting nerve cells. Based on this information, the brain decides what instructions to send out to different parts of the body.

In most animals, the brain has deep folds that give it a large surface area. Like the spinal cord, the brain is wrapped in three tough membranes and contains a fluid that helps absorb shocks.

Your brain consists of billions of brain cells. Because many of them work most of the time, they need a lot of energy and a lot of oxygen. The rich supply of blood to the brain keeps these nerve cells healthy.

The brain is divided into different regions. One region, the medulla, is the control center for breathing and the heartbeat. Another region, the cerebellum, helps coordinate movements and control balance.

The hypothalamus receives information from the heart, lungs, kidneys, and stomach and helps control these organs. It also controls some of the activities of the pituitary gland. Near the hypothalamus is the thalamus, the central relay-station for almost all information entering and leaving the cerebrum.

In some animals the cerebrum is the largest part of the brain. It contains sensory areas that receive information from the face, tongue, throat, arms, legs, and skin. It also contains motor areas that send out instructions to control face, arm, and leg muscles. These skeletal muscles can be willingly controlled. Nerve cells in the cerebrum are also responsible for learning, memory, thought, and emotions.

Nerves on the left side of the brain communicate with those on the right side through bridges of interconnecting nerves, called the corpus callosum.

Nerve cells that control activities such as breathing have to work even when animals aren't awake. But when animals are asleep, their brain cells work at a slower rate.

The complicated nerve connections in the brain are responsible for the way animals behave. But little is known about how the brain does so many things at the same time.

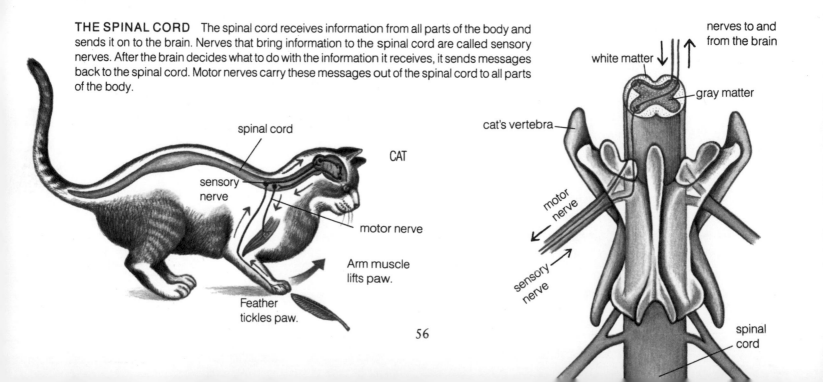

THE SPINAL CORD The spinal cord receives information from all parts of the body and sends it on to the brain. Nerves that bring information to the spinal cord are called sensory nerves. After the brain decides what to do with the information it receives, it sends messages back to the spinal cord. Motor nerves carry these messages out of the spinal cord to all parts of the body.

spinal cord

CAT

sensory nerve

motor nerve

Arm muscle lifts paw.

Feather tickles paw.

nerves to and from the brain

white matter

gray matter

cat's vertebra

motor nerve

sensory nerve

spinal cord

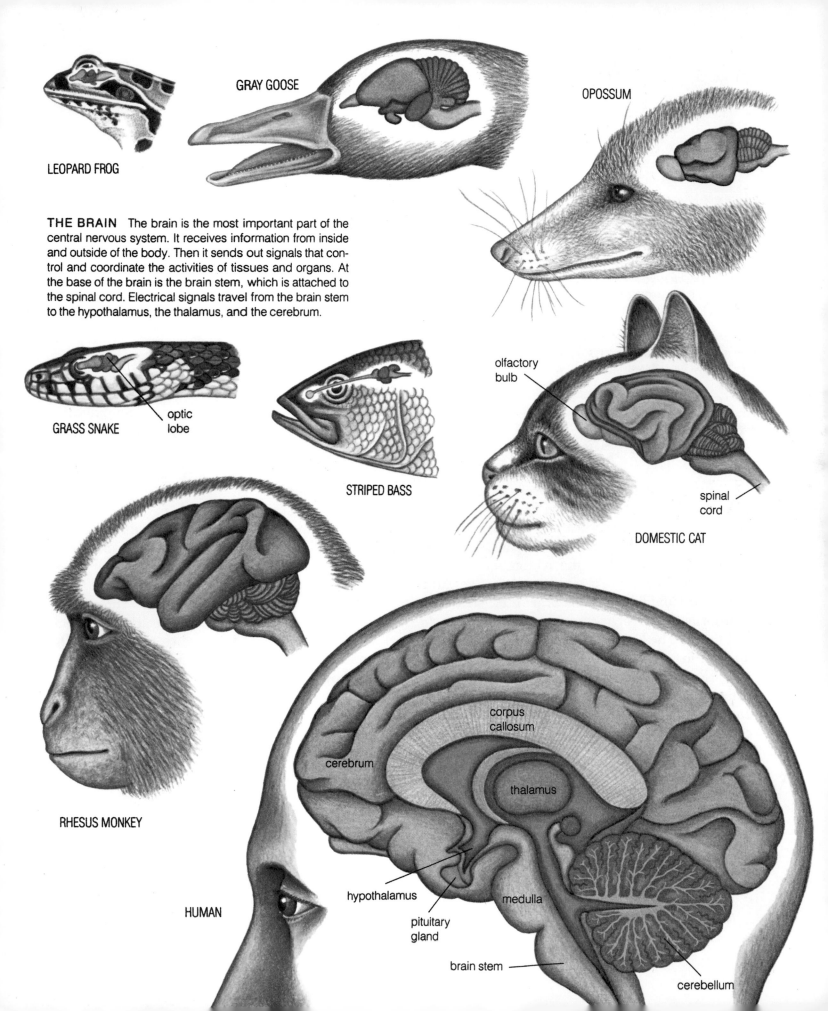

LEOPARD FROG

GRAY GOOSE

OPOSSUM

THE BRAIN The brain is the most important part of the central nervous system. It receives information from inside and outside of the body. Then it sends out signals that control and coordinate the activities of tissues and organs. At the base of the brain is the brain stem, which is attached to the spinal cord. Electrical signals travel from the brain stem to the hypothalamus, the thalamus, and the cerebrum.

GRASS SNAKE

optic lobe

STRIPED BASS

olfactory bulb

spinal cord

DOMESTIC CAT

RHESUS MONKEY

HUMAN

corpus callosum

cerebrum

thalamus

hypothalamus

pituitary gland

medulla

brain stem

cerebellum

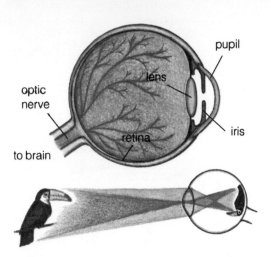

YOUR EYE Light enters your eye through the pupil, an opening in the colored iris. The image the light is carrying is focused on your retina by your lens. The image is converted into electrical signals, which are carried by the optic nerve to the seeing areas in your brain. Your brain puts the picture together the right way.

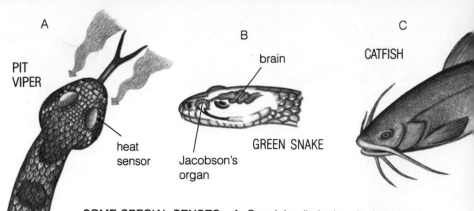

SOME SPECIAL SENSES A. Special cells in the pit viper's head sense the heat given off by living things. B. A snake's tongue picks up chemical particles from the ground or air and carries them to Jacobson's organ. This organ reacts to odors and helps the snake trail its prey. C. Cells in the lateral line organ sense motion in the water, alerting fish to danger or food. D. Hairs on the legs of web-building spiders pick up movements when something is caught in the web. E. Bats locate insects and other objects by giving off very high-pitched sound waves. When these waves bounce off objects, they are picked up by the bat's ears and help it to figure out exactly where the object is.

The Senses

Animals have to pick up information from their surroundings to help them find food, water, a mate, the safest place to live, and the fastest way to escape from danger. Special sense organs, such as the eye and ear, collect this information and change it into electrical signals that are carried by nerves to the spinal cord and brain. In the brain these signals are transformed into sight, hearing, taste, smell, pain, and touch. The brain decides what to do with this information and how an animal will react.

Sense organs contain receptor cells. Receptor cells in the eye respond to light and color. Those in the ear are sensitive to sound vibrations. In the nose, receptor cells react to odors in the air.

Skin picks up information through different kinds of nerves that respond to touch, pressure, heat, and cold. The nerves in skin can also sense pain. Pain is a warning signal that cells are being damaged and that it is necessary to get away from whatever is causing the pain. Animals without skin often have hairs on their body surface that are sensitive to touch.

Smell and Taste

Many animals, such as wolves and lions, depend upon their sense of smell to locate their food. Smells come from chemical molecules that are picked up by tiny hairs on the olfactory or smell membrane, in the nasal cavity. These hairs react to chemicals and stimulate nerve cells to carry information about these chemicals to the olfactory areas in the brain.

Most animals taste their food when it enters their mouth. Insects, however, have taste cells not only on their mouth parts but also on their legs. Taste cells respond to chemical molecules in food by letting the brain know which are sweet, bitter, salty, or sour.

Sight

Animals use their eyes to see the world around them. Light waves carry information into the eyes, where it is converted into electrical signals and sent to the seeing areas in the brain. When light waves hit objects, they reflect (bounce off) the objects. It is these reflected waves that carry patterns and images to the eyes.

Light enters your eye through the pupil, an opening in the colored iris. The iris regulates the amount of light entering the eye by changing the size of the pupil. The light then passes through the lens, which

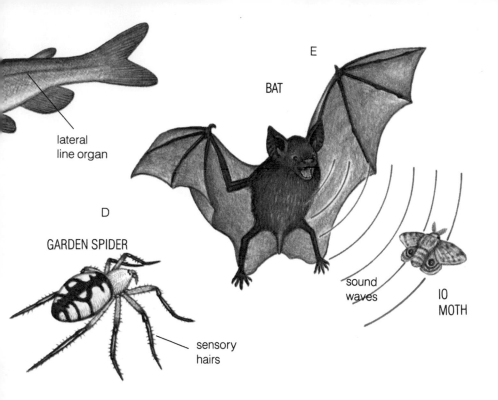

lateral
line organ

E

BAT

D

GARDEN SPIDER

sensory
hairs

sound
waves

IO
MOTH

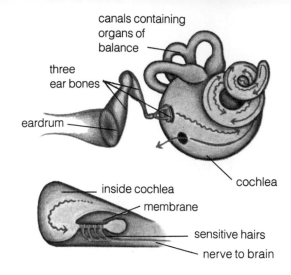

canals containing
organs of
balance

three
ear bones

eardrum

cochlea

inside cochlea

membrane

sensitive hairs

nerve to brain

YOUR EAR Sound waves cause your eardrum to vibrate. Three tiny bones pick up these vibrations and carry them to your inner ear, or cochlea. The inner ear contains fluid-filled tubes lined with stiff fibers. When these hairs move, they cause special cells to send electrical signals to the hearing parts of your brain.

is composed of transparent protein fibers. Just as a camera lens focuses an image on film, the lens in the eye focuses an image on the retina.

The retina, located at the back of the eye, receives the image carried by the light waves. But the lens has turned this image upside down and reversed it. Only the brain can put it back the right way.

The retina contains rod-shaped cells that are important for seeing in dim light. It also contains cone-shaped cells that react to colors. The rod and cone cells transmit the entire image to nerve cells at the back of the eye. These nerve cells send electrical signals along the optic nerve to the seeing areas in the brain.

Not all animals have the same kind of eyes as you do. The eyes of crabs, shrimp, and insects are made up of thousands of cylinder-shaped units. Each unit is like a camera, picking up light waves and changing them into electrical signals, which are then sent to the brain.

Hearing

Sounds produce waves in the air, causing the air to vibrate. Your ears capture these sound waves and funnel them into the hearing or auditory canal. At the end of this canal is the eardrum, a thin, stretched membrane that vibrates exactly like the sound waves hitting it. Attached to the eardrum from the inside is a bone that looks like a hammer. It also vibrates and causes other ear bones to vibrate too. These bones carry the vibrations to your inner ear.

Your inner ear, or cochlea, is made up of coiled tubes filled with fluid. These tubes are separated from each other by membranes containing stiff, hairlike fibers. When the vibrations reach the fluid, the fluid picks up the waves and moves the sensitive hairs. These hairs touch cells that change the vibrations into electrical signals, which are then carried to the hearing areas in your brain.

Balance

Your inner ear has additional fluid-filled canals containing the organs of balance. These organs send signals to the brain that help you keep your balance when you are moving. If you lose your balance these organs send signals to the cerebellum, which uses the information to help you regain your balance.

The song of the whale bounces for miles beneath the surface of the water.

FINBACK WHALE

FIREFLY

BABY CHICK

Birds use their songs to identify themselves, attract mates, sound alarms, and tell other birds to stay away from their territory. When a baby chick is in trouble, it will peep for its mother.

OVENBIRD

Fireflies identify themselves by the pattern and color of the light flashes they give off.

After an ant scout finds food, it gives off a chemical trail that other ants follow. If an ant senses danger, it gives off an alarm chemical that alerts the rest of the ants to the threat.

LITTLE
BLACK ANT

PRAIRIE DOGS

The discus cichlid becomes darker when it is disturbed. The bright color of this frog lets other animals know it is poisonous.

Prairie dogs greet each other with kisses. Kissing is a way one prairie dog recognizes a member of its group.

POISON FROG

DISCUS CICHLID

When honeybee scouts find food, they return to their hive and begin to dance. If they dance around in circles (A), they are telling worker bees that food is near the hive. If they do a waggle dance (B,C,D), they are telling worker bees the direction and distance of food located far from the hive. A waggle straight up (B) means fly in the direction of the Sun to find food. A waggle in the other direction (C) means fly away from the Sun. A waggle at the angle in picture D means fly at that angle to the left of the Sun. The number of turns a bee makes tells how far the food is from the hive. The fewer the turns, the farther away the food.

A   B   C   D

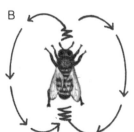
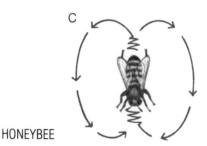
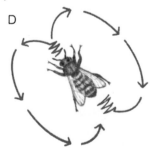
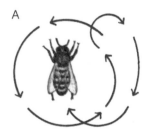

HONEYBEE

MANDRILL BABOON

The look on the mandrill's face warns animals to stay away.

PRAIRIE CHICKEN

During the mating season the male prairie chicken runs back and forth with his wings drooping and his neck up. As he runs he makes deep sounds. All of these signals tell female chickens he is ready to mate.

WOLF PUPS

By giving off the correct signals, one animal lets another animal know that it wants to play. When a male wolf pup raises its tail, the female rolls on her back and raises her paw. This is an invitation to play.

Communication

A nimals have many ways of communicating with each other. They make sounds, give off scents, move, touch each other, give off light signals, and change colors. They let each other know what group they belong to and where they are located. They also warn other animals to stay away from them and, when necessary, they make it clear that they will fight if they have to. There are signals that mean danger is near, help is needed, that animals are hungry or just want to play. Attracting a mate often requires sending out the right signals at the right time.

Animals can communicate detailed information to each other. One of the most amazing examples of this is how honeybees tell each other where to find food. Honeybee scouts are sent out from the hive in search of food. When a scout finds food, it collects samples of pollen and nectar and brings them back to the hive. In order to let the worker bees know where the food is, the scout begins to "dance" on the surface of the honeycomb.

If the food is close to the hive, the scout's dance consists of making circles to the left and to the right again and again. A long dance signals that a lot of food has been discovered. In response to this dance, other bees imitate the dancer as it moves and pick up the food scent from its body. Then they fly out close to the hive in search of the food.

If the food is far from the hive, the returning scout does a more complicated dance. The steps in this dance produce figure eights. First the scout runs in a straight line, moving its body from side to side. Then it makes a half-circle and runs forward again, waggling its body. Then it makes another half-circle in the opposite direction. The number of turns the dancing bee makes tells how far away the food is. A few turns means the food is far from the hive. A lot of turns means it is closer.

The waggle part of the dance tells the worker bees in which direction to fly. Bees use the position of the Sun to help them locate their food. If, during the waggle, the bee runs straight up the honeycomb surface, this means food is in the direction of the Sun. If it runs at an angle, this means that food can be found at that angle from the Sun. From this dance, the worker bees know exactly where to find food.

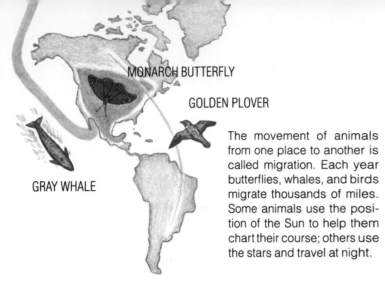

MONARCH BUTTERFLY

GOLDEN PLOVER

GRAY WHALE

The movement of animals from one place to another is called migration. Each year butterflies, whales, and birds migrate thousands of miles. Some animals use the position of the Sun to help them chart their course; others use the stars and travel at night.

ROOSTER

MORNING GLORY

Many animals and plants behave as if they can tell what time it is. Roosters will crow at sunrise, and morning glories close in the afternoon.

When it is time for them to mate, salmon swim from the ocean to the same freshwater stream where they were hatched.

SALMON

Finding the Way

Like honeybee scouts, many animals have to find their way home after they have found food. Some animals use rocks, trees, and other landmarks to help them locate their homes. Others give off chemicals that mark a route back to their nests.

During their lives most animals move, or migrate, from one place to another. Some animals never return to the same places, and others have such a keen sense of direction that they can return to the exact spot they left months or even years before.

Each year birds, butterflies, whales, salmon, and many other animals migrate hundreds, even thousands of miles to specific destinations. Salmon, for example, hatch from eggs in freshwater streams. At age two they swim to the ocean and live there for a few years. When the time comes for them to reproduce, each salmon has to find its way back to the place where it was born. Even though this return trip may be more than 2,000 miles (3,200 kilometers), some salmon make the long trip back to their hatching place, where they can mate.

The digger wasp flies around her nest to learn the position of rocks and trees. She uses these landmarks to find her way home.

DIGGER WASP

Dolphins send out sound waves that bounce off objects in the water and echo back to the dolphin. These sound waves give the dolphin information about the size of objects and where they are located.

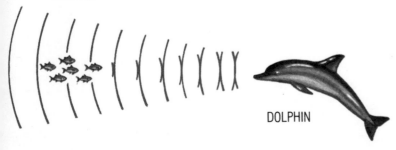

DOLPHIN

Chipmunks are most active during the day. Other animals, such as owls, come out at night.

OWL

CHIPMUNK

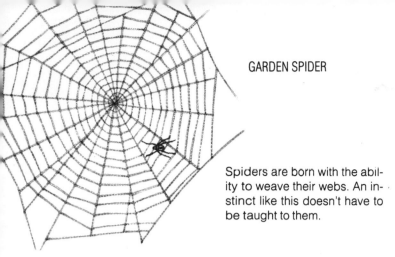

GARDEN SPIDER

Spiders are born with the ability to weave their webs. An instinct like this doesn't have to be taught to them.

At first, chicks are afraid of falling leaves. But once they learn that leaves are not dangerous, they are no longer afraid.

QUAIL CHICKS

Learning

Spiders are born with the knowledge of how to spin a web. Bees build their hives and birds construct their nests without being taught how to do it. Anything an animal is born knowing how to do is called an instinct.

Animals don't have to rely only on their instincts, for they are also able to learn. Learning involves storing information in the memory and being able to use it when it is needed. For example, adult animals learn to recognize their young. This is very important because in large groups where there are many young animals, parents have to pick out their own hungry children and keep them well fed.

Learning usually causes a change in the way an animal behaves. At first, birds are afraid of scarecrows. But after a while they become used to them because they have learned that there is no reason to be afraid.

Some animals also learn to use objects as tools. Chimpanzees, for example, use sticks as levers and weapons and as tools for catching insects.

opened nut

By trial and error, squirrels learn the fastest way to get at a nut inside a shell.

SQUIRREL

After being stung once, a toad learns a painful lesson — don't try to eat bumblebees.

FOWLER'S TOAD   BUMBLEBEE

These newborn geese are following the first moving object they see, which in this case is a duck. They become permanently attached to this duck and treat her like their mother.

CANADA GOSLINGS

TEAL DUCK

The sea otter uses a stone to crack open mussel shells. While floating on its back, the otter smashes the shells against the stone until they open.

SEA OTTER

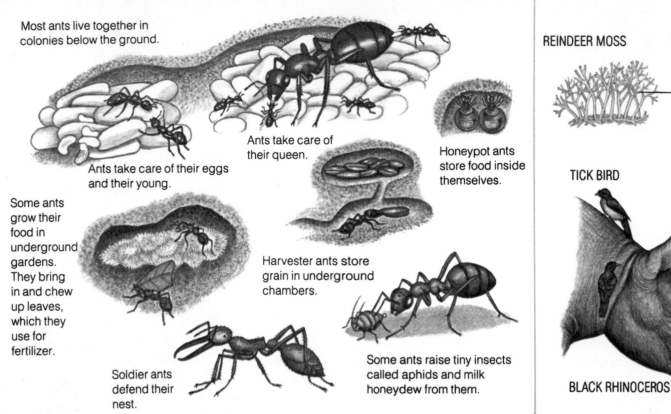

Most ants live together in colonies below the ground.

Ants take care of their eggs and their young.

Ants take care of their queen.

Honeypot ants store food inside themselves.

Some ants grow their food in underground gardens. They bring in and chew up leaves, which they use for fertilizer.

Harvester ants store grain in underground chambers.

Soldier ants defend their nest.

Some ants raise tiny insects called aphids and milk honeydew from them.

REINDEER MOSS

ALGA

FUNGUS

Lichens are an alga and a fungus living together.

TICK BIRD

BLACK RHINOCEROS

Living Together

Most animals spend at least part of their lives living in a group. There are flocks of birds, herds of animals, and schools of fish. By forming a group, animals can protect each other, and by hunting together, they often have a better chance of capturing food. In winter they stay warm by huddling next to each other.

Ant Societies

There are about one million billion ants living on Earth. Most of these ants live in colonies below the ground. Each colony is ruled by a queen, who lays the eggs that develop into worker and soldier ants.

Workers have many jobs to do. They build and repair the nest. Some gather food; others feed and care for the queen. Workers also have to take care of the young until they develop into adults. Each nest is defended by the worker and soldier ants.

There are many different types of ant societies. In one of these societies ants live by stealing the eggs and larvae from other ant nests. They carry their captives back to their home, where they sometimes make them into slaves.

Army ants travel in troops searching for food. An army ant community can contain hundreds of thousands of ants all working together as they move their camp from one place to another.

Leaf-cutting ants eat proteins found in certain types of fungus (page 71). Often these fungi will only grow in underground gardens built by the ants. The smallest ants take care of these gardens. Larger ants go out of the nest, cut off sections from leaves, and carry them back to the nest. There the leaves are first chewed and then put in the garden as fertilizer for the growing fungi. The largest worker ants stand guard, ready to defend the nest and its gardens.

Symbiosis

Sometimes two different kinds of organisms live with each other in a close way. The relationships that they form are often permanent and are called symbiotic. "Symbiosis" means "living together."

Both animals can benefit from some symbiotic relationships. Tick birds, for example, ride on the backs of rhinoceroses and eat the ticks that live in the rhinoceroses' skin. The rhinoceroses benefit from this arrangement by getting rid of the annoying ticks, and

Some organisms live in a close way with a different kind of organism. When the tick bird eats ticks living in the rhinoceros's skin, both animals benefit. But when the cuckoo bird hatches in the nest of another smaller bird, it shoves out all of the other bird's babies and takes all of the food for itself.

Mistletoe steals nutrients from other plants.

MISTLETOE

CUCKOO BIRD

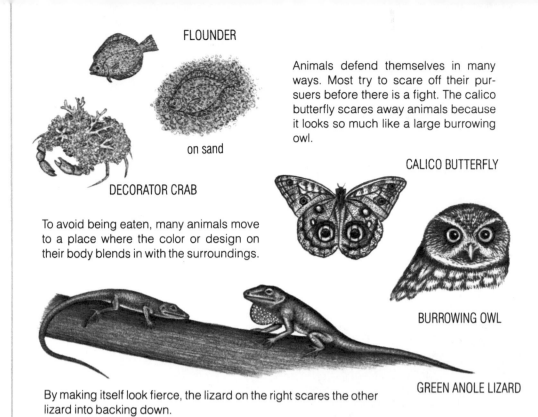

FLOUNDER

on sand

DECORATOR CRAB

To avoid being eaten, many animals move to a place where the color or design on their body blends in with the surroundings.

Animals defend themselves in many ways. Most try to scare off their pursuers before there is a fight. The calico butterfly scares away animals because it looks so much like a large burrowing owl.

CALICO BUTTERFLY

BURROWING OWL

GREEN ANOLE LIZARD

By making itself look fierce, the lizard on the right scares the other lizard into backing down.

---

the tick birds benefit by getting food.

A lichen is a type of plant that is really an alga and a fungus living together. By photosynthesis, the alga produces food for the fungus, and the fungus takes in the water and minerals needed by the alga.

In another form of symbiosis, called parasitism, one animal or plant benefits from a relationship and the other is harmed by it. The plant or animal causing the harm is called the parasite; the victim is called the host. Parasites live off their hosts, either inside or outside the hosts' bodies. Many disease-producing organisms, such as tapeworms (page 72), live inside their hosts. The dodder plant lives outside its host plant and steals water and minerals from it.

A baby European cuckoo bird becomes a parasite when its mother lays her egg in the nest of another, smaller bird. When it hatches, the baby cuckoo lives off the food brought to it by the bird that made the nest. Because it grows quickly, the young cuckoo is able to shove the smaller bird's babies out of the nest so it can get all of the food.

Self-defense

Whether animals live alone, in groups, or with another kind of animal, they all have to protect themselves from being killed by other animals for food. When attacked, an animal will do everything possible to save itself. It depends on its nervous system to coordinate all of the activities necessary for it to react to the attack. In many animals, one of these activities is producing a hormone called adrenaline, which causes more sugar to be carried by the blood to the heart and skeletal muscles. Extra energy is instantly available so the animal can make its move. Some quickly escape from danger; others remain and fight for their lives.

Animals often avoid being caught by fooling their hungry pursuers. Some move to areas where their body colors and patterns blend into the surroundings. This camouflage makes them difficult to detect. Many small animals scare off hungry predators by making themselves look like larger animals or by resembling poisonous animals.

Most animals have an area, or territory, that they will defend against intruders. When an intruder approaches, an animal will send out clear signals that it will fight to defend its territory if it has to. Most of the time a fight does not take place because one animal backs down.

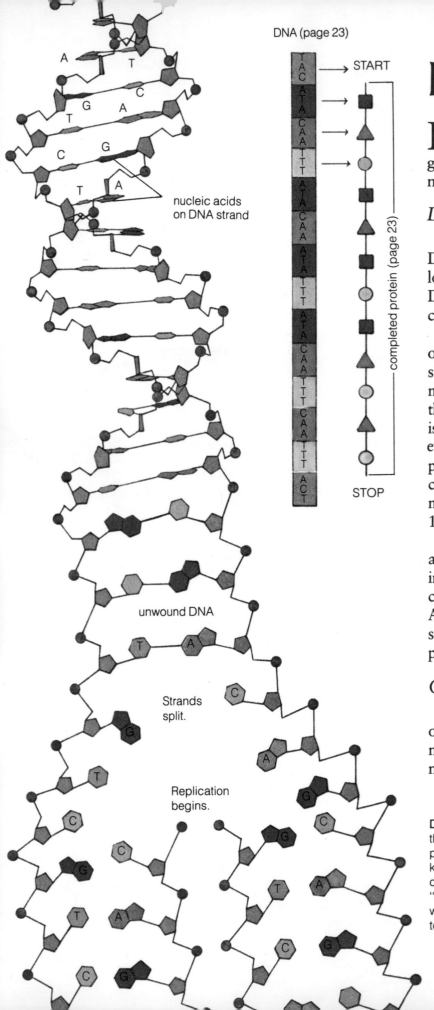

DNA (page 23)

START

STOP

completed protein (page 23)

nucleic acids
on DNA strand

unwound DNA

Strands split.

Replication begins.

Blueprints for Life

Every plant and animal begins life as a single cell that contains all of the information it needs to grow and develop. This information is carried by molecules of DNA.

DNA

DNA is deoxyribonucleic acid. Each molecule of DNA consists of nucleic acids linked together into long strands. There are four kinds of nucleic acids in DNA: adenine (A), thymine (T), guanine (G), and cytosine (C).

Every molecule of DNA is made up of two strands of nucleic acids that twist around each other like the steps in a spiral staircase. At each "step" on the DNA molecule, there is a pair of nucleic acids. Wherever there is an adenine (A) on one half of the step, there is a thymine (T) on the other, and vice versa. Wherever there is a cytosine (C), there is a guanine (G). By pairing A with T and G with C, weak bonds are created that help hold the two strands together. DNA molecules can be very long and contain more than 100 million nucleic acids.

The information needed to make every protein in a cell is contained in the DNA of that cell. This information is spelled out in a very simple chemical code. How this code works is illustrated on this page. As you can see, the order of the nucleic acids on a strand is very important because it determines how a protein will be made (page 23).

Chromosomes

Bacteria and other simple organisms usually have only one molecule of DNA. But most plant and animal cells have more than one molecule of DNA in the nucleus to carry all of the information they need.

DNA In the nucleus of a cell, DNA molecules like this one on the left carry the blueprints for making proteins and other cell parts. These blueprints are in a chemical code that uses four kinds of nucleic acids: adenine (A), thymine (T), guanine (G), and cytosine (C). Three nucleic acids in a row on a strand spell out the "words" in the code. As shown above, these "words" indicate where to start making the protein, where to stop, and how to link together the amino acids in the protein.

Each separate molecule of DNA is protected by special proteins. Together they form a chromosome. Cat cells have a total of 32 chromosomes, dog cells have 78, a carrot cell has 18, and your cells have 46.

Making More Cells

Cells reproduce by dividing into two identical cells, called daughter cells. In order for the daughter cells to be identical, each has to have a complete set of DNA molecules, which contain the blueprints to make all of the cell parts. For this reason, a cell must make a copy of each of its chromosomes before it can begin to divide.

Replication

The process of making duplicate copies of DNA molecules is called replication. When replication begins, a special protein starts unwinding a DNA molecule. As the DNA unwinds, the strands split down the middle and separate. This process is shown at the bottom of the DNA molecule illustrated on the opposite page.

As you can see, next to the open strand on the right, a new DNA strand starts to form. Special enzymes put this strand together by lining up adenine next to thymine and guanine next to cytosine. The same thing happens next to the open strand on the left. This process continues until the entire DNA molecule has been copied.

When replication is completed, the two copies do not separate from each other. Instead, a ringlike structure, called a centromere, holds the copies together while the cell prepares to divide.

Mitosis

The first part of cell division is called mitosis. During mitosis the nuclear membranes dissolve and the duplicated chromosomes line up in the center of the cell. Then special fibers pull the copies apart from each other, creating two identical sets of DNA molecules. After these sets separate from each other, a new nucleus forms around each set.

During the second part of cell division, called cytokinesis, the middle of the cell pinches together and finally splits into two daughter cells.

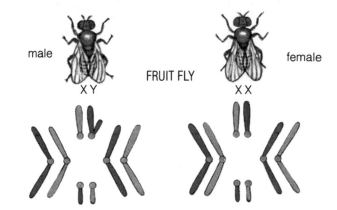

male   FRUIT FLY   female

CHROMOSOMES These brother and sister fruit flies have 8 chromosomes in the nucleus of their cells. Four came from their father (red) and 4 from their mother (green). The X and the Y chromosomes are the sex chromosomes.

nucleus   chromosome

MITOSIS Before a cell divides, it makes a copy of each of its chromosomes. Each copy is joined to the original chromosome by a centromere.

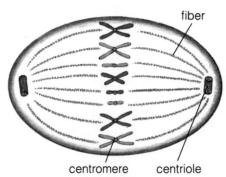

fiber

During mitosis two centrioles move to opposite sides of the cell and the nuclear membranes dissolve. The duplicated chromosomes line up in the center of the cell. Fibers stretch from each centriole, attach to the centromeres, and pull the copies apart, forming two complete sets.

centromere   centriole

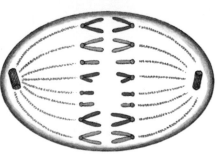

A new nucleus forms around each set of chromosomes. Then the middle of the cell pinches together until the cell splits into two identical daughter cells.

nucleus   nucleus

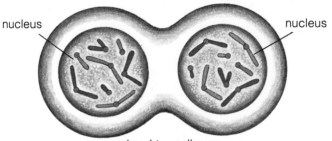

daughter cells

67

Your DNA

You started life as a single cell inside your mother's body. That cell contained 46 chromosomes. Twenty-three of those chromosomes came from your father and 23 came from your mother. The chromosomes from your father contained his set of instructions for making all of the parts of your body. Those from your mother contained her set of instructions for making the same parts.

When you began to develop, the single cell divided into two identical cells. Then each of those cells divided, making four cells. This process continued until your body had millions of cells when you were born. Inside the nucleus of every one of those cells there was a copy of the complete set of 46 chromosomes.

As you developed inside your mother, a point was reached when your cells started to become different from each other. Some cells became muscle cells; some became nerve cells; others formed your stomach. Cells continued to become different from each other until you had every kind of tissue and organ your body needed.

The cells in your body were able to become different from each other because each kind of cell could select from your 46 chromosomes the information it needed to carry on its work. Cells in your pancreas, for example, used the information on how to make insulin molecules. None of the other cells in your body use this information even though it is present in the DNA molecules in every cell.

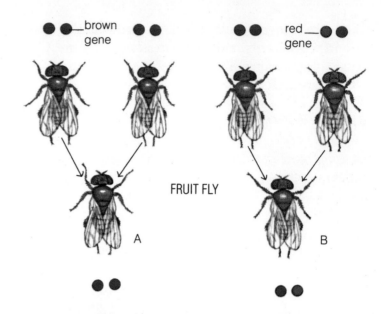

Genes

A cell can select exactly the information it needs from its DNA molecules because chromosomes are divided into sections, called genes. Each gene contains the blueprint for making one kind of molecule. There are separate genes for hemoglobin, for pepsin, for antibodies, and for every hormone. Genes line up on chromosomes like train stations on railroad lines. Just as train stations can be put on a map, it is possible to map out where different genes are located on your chromosomes.

Two Sets of Instructions

The genes you received from each of your parents can sometimes carry the same instructions. For example, if you have blue eyes, then you received one gene for blue eyes from your father and one gene for blue eyes from your mother.

The genes can also carry different instructions. If you received one gene for blue eyes from your father and one gene for brown eyes from your mother, your eyes would be brown. The gene for brown eyes is

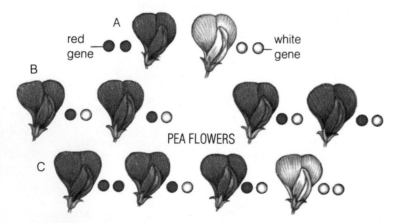

When a pea plant with red flowers reproduces with a pea plant with white flowers (A) all of the flowers are red (B). When two of these plants with red flowers (B) reproduce (C), three quarters of the new plants have red flowers and one quarter have white.

68

called a dominant gene because it shows itself. The gene for blue eyes is called a recessive gene because even though it was in your DNA, it didn't have a chance to show itself.

Two of the chromosomes you received from your parents (one from each parent) determined your sex. Sex chromosomes are called either X or Y chromosomes. If you are a girl, you have two X chromosomes in each of your cells. If you are a boy, you have one X and one Y chromosome in your cells. Males always receive their Y chromosome from their father and their X chromosome from their mother. Females get one X chromosome from each parent.

Meiosis

When you become an adult and decide to have your own children, you will pass on your genes to them. But you can't pass on all 46 of your chromosomes because your children's cells would then have too many chromosomes. Your body produces special cells that have only 23 chromosomes. Males produce sperm cells to carry their 23 chromosomes, and females produce egg cells to carry their 23 chromosomes.

Your body produces sperm cells or egg cells by the process of meiosis. Some of the steps in this process are shown below. During meiosis, two cell divisions take place instead of one. Each egg cell or sperm cell produced during meiosis carries one complete set of DNA instructions contained in 23 chromosomes. But this set is not the entire set you got from your father, nor is it the entire set you got from your mother. Instead it is some of the chromosomes from your father and some from your mother. During meiosis your chromosomes mix up and separate into many different combinations.

More of the Same

All living things reproduce. Reproduction means making more of the same kind of living thing. Very simple organisms reproduce by dividing into two identical cells. Many other organisms produce sperm and egg cells to carry their DNA molecules from one generation to the next. Any time reproduction involves two parents, both parents have to be the same kind, or species, of animal or plant. Only if they are of the same species will both the male and female have the right blueprints in their DNA molecules for making their kind of offspring.

MEIOSIS Sperm cells and egg cells are produced by the process of meiosis. In this illustration, four sperm cells will develop from the cell on the left (step 1). Only two pairs of chromosomes are shown in this cell. One pair is the sex chromosomes, X and Y. The other pair carries genes for eye color. One gene is for brown eyes, the other for blue eyes. In step 2 a copy of each chromosome is made and held to the original by a centromere. During the first cell division of meiosis (step 3) the pairs separate. During the second cell division (step 4) the copies separate. Each of the cells in step 5 become sperm cells. During reproduction one sperm cell will penetrate the egg cell on the right. If it is a sperm with an X chromosome, the baby will be a girl with brown eyes. If it is a sperm cell with a Y chromosome, the baby will be a boy with blue eyes.

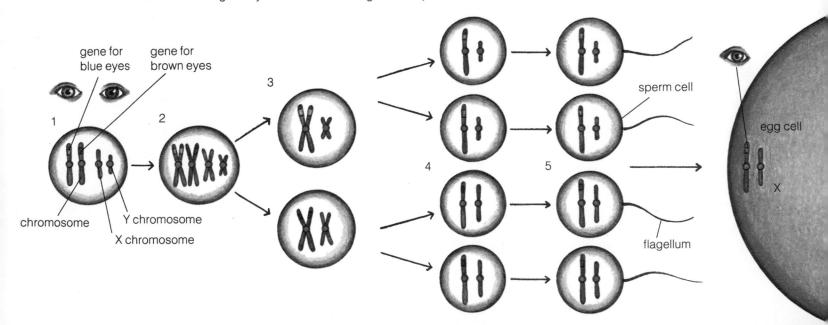

gene for blue eyes   gene for brown eyes

1   2   3   4   5

chromosome   Y chromosome   X chromosome

sperm cell   egg cell   X   flagellum

BACTERIAL CELL

Chromosome duplicates.

chromosome

daughter cells

FROM ONE INTO TWO Bacteria make a copy of their chromosome, then divide by binary fission into two identical cells.

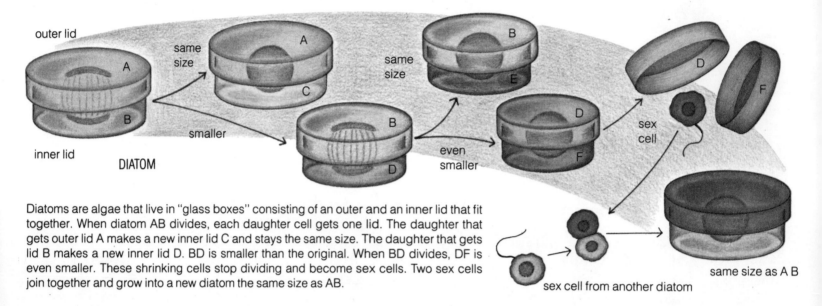

outer lid

same size

A

A

C

B

E

same size

inner lid

smaller

DIATOM

B

D

even smaller

D

F

sex cell

D

F

same size as A B

sex cell from another diatom

Diatoms are algae that live in "glass boxes" consisting of an outer and an inner lid that fit together. When diatom AB divides, each daughter cell gets one lid. The daughter that gets outer lid A makes a new inner lid C and stays the same size. The daughter that gets lid B makes a new inner lid D. BD is smaller than the original. When BD divides, DF is even smaller. These shrinking cells stop dividing and become sex cells. Two sex cells join together and grow into a new diatom the same size as AB.

Reproducing Life

Bacteria are the smallest single-celled organisms. Many are shaped like rods, cylinders, or ovals. Some bacteria cause diseases, but most don't. Bacteria usually have a single circular chromosome. Before a bacterium divides, a copy of this chromosome is made. After this copy separates from the original, a groove forms near the center of the cell and cuts the cell into two identical daughter cells. This process, called binary fission, is a form of asexual reproduction. The DNA from only one parent cell is involved in asexual reproduction.

Algae

The smallest plantlike organisms are called algae. Like plant cells, algae carry on photosynthesis. Some algae live as single cells; others join together to form colonies. Algae grow in soil, in fresh water, and in salt water. Some algae survive in very cold places; others can live in 158°F. (70°C.) hot springs.

There are blue-green, yellow, red, and brown algae. The Red Sea gets its color from the red algae growing in it. In these different-colored algae, the chemicals that produce their colors take in energy from light and pass this energy on to chlorophyll molecules. Fifty percent of all the oxygen produced on Earth during photosynthesis comes from algae.

Diatoms are the most common type of algae. They live in "glass boxes." Each box consists of an inner lid and an outer lid that fit together. Both lids are made of colorless, jellylike pectin and glassy silica.

When diatoms divide asexually, each new cell gets a copy of the DNA molecules and one half of the glass box. The new cell that gets the large outer lid makes a new inner one and remains the same size. The other new cell, which gets the smaller lid, also makes a new inner lid. But this cell is smaller than the parent. After many divisions, the shrinking cells get to be too small. They stop dividing asexually and turn into sex cells. They grow taillike flagella after throwing off their glass boxes and swim in search of another sex cell. When two sex cells find each other, they join together and combine the DNA molecules in their nuclei. The new diatom that they form grows to the original large size. Sex cells take part in sexual reproduction, which always involves combining the DNA molecules from two parent cells into one new cell.

Fungi

Mushrooms, molds, yeasts, and the single cells that produce penicillin are all fungi. Although some fungi, such as mushrooms, look like plants, they aren't—fungus cells don't have chlorophyll and can't make their own food. Fungi get their nutrients either by stealing them from other living cells or by absorbing their food from the remains of dead plants and animals. When fungi break up dead matter, they help recycle elements such as carbon.

Mushrooms

The body of a mushroom, called a mycelium, is made up of thin threads that lie below the ground. These threads grow in all directions, giving off enzymes that break down material from dead plants and animals.

The umbrella-shaped part of the mushroom grows above the ground, but only after sexual reproduction has taken place underground. During sexual reproduction, reproductive threads from two mushrooms have to meet in the soil. Then they join together to create one new cell that contains the DNA from each thread. This new cell divides and grows into the mushroom you see growing above the ground.

Early in its development, this mushroom is enclosed in a thin tissue. At first the mushroom looks like a small white button, but as it grows, the thin tissue tears and the stalk emerges from it. The umbrella-shaped mushroom cap grows on top of the stalk. It is lined with gills (not like fish gills) that hang next to each other. Each gill contains cells that make tiny spores. Spores carry the DNA blueprints for making more mushroom bodies underground.

When spores are mature, they are released into the space between two gills. Some fall to the ground, but most are so light that they are picked up by the wind and carried away. One mushroom can release millions of spores every day for several days in a row. Although every spore can grow into a new mushroom, most don't because they land in places where conditions aren't right for growing. Spores need moisture and the proper temperature before they can burst open and start to grow.

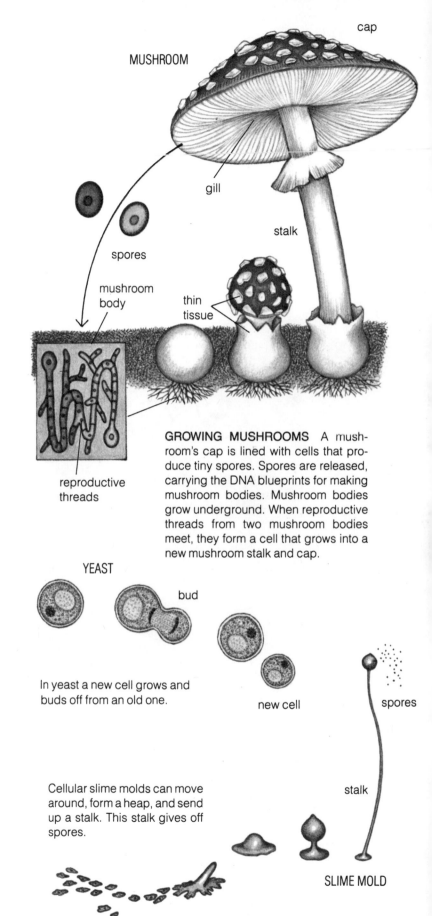

GROWING MUSHROOMS A mushroom's cap is lined with cells that produce tiny spores. Spores are released, carrying the DNA blueprints for making mushroom bodies. Mushroom bodies grow underground. When reproductive threads from two mushroom bodies meet, they form a cell that grows into a new mushroom stalk and cap.

In yeast a new cell grows and buds off from an old one.

Cellular slime molds can move around, form a heap, and send up a stalk. This stalk gives off spores.

71

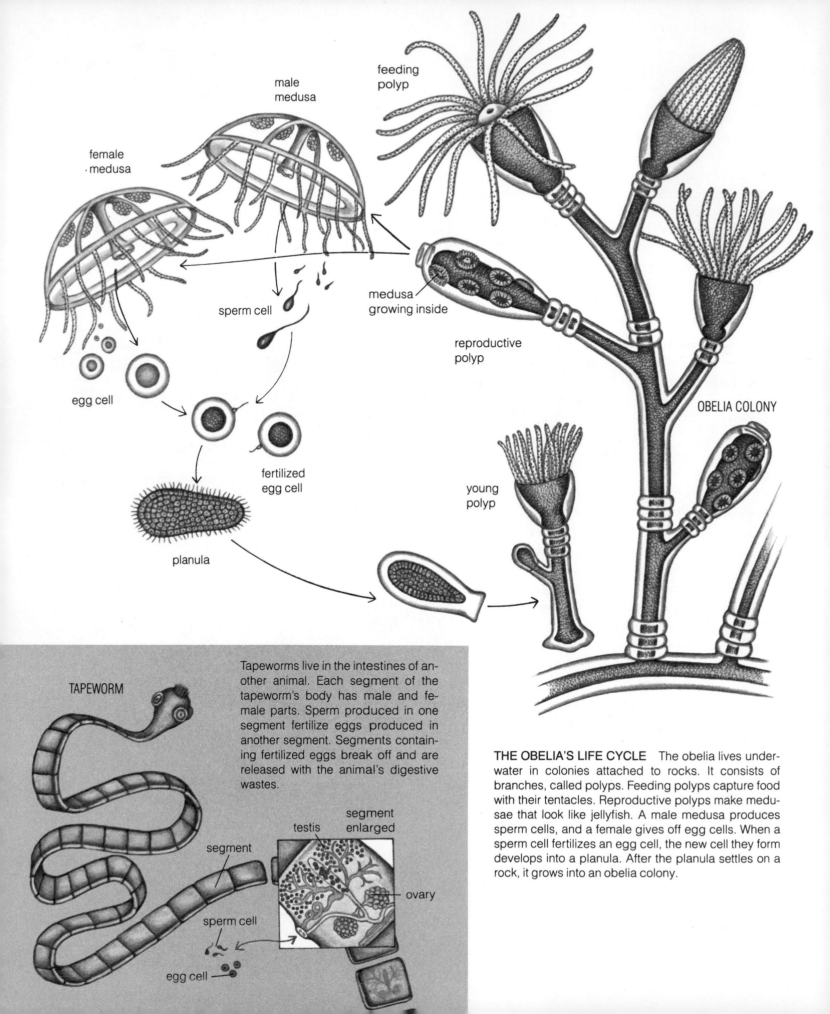

feeding
polyp

male
medusa

female
medusa

sperm cell

medusa
growing inside

reproductive
polyp

egg cell

fertilized
egg cell

OBELIA COLONY

planula

young
polyp

TAPEWORM

Tapeworms live in the intestines of another animal. Each segment of the tapeworm's body has male and female parts. Sperm produced in one segment fertilize eggs produced in another segment. Segments containing fertilized eggs break off and are released with the animal's digestive wastes.

segment
enlarged

testis

segment

ovary

sperm cell

egg cell

THE OBELIA'S LIFE CYCLE The obelia lives underwater in colonies attached to rocks. It consists of branches, called polyps. Feeding polyps capture food with their tentacles. Reproductive polyps make medusae that look like jellyfish. A male medusa produces sperm cells, and a female gives off egg cells. When a sperm cell fertilizes an egg cell, the new cell they form develops into a planula. After the planula settles on a rock, it grows into an obelia colony.

Life Cycles

The obelia is an animal that lives underwater in colonies attached to rocks and other objects. Each colony starts life as a single cell that divides and grows. As it develops, the obelia buds off branches, called polyps. Some of these polyps, called feeding polyps, consist of a mouth surrounded by tentacles. Other polyps help it to reproduce. All of the polyps are connected to a central cavity in which food circulates to all of the animal's cells.

The obelia's reproductive polyps produce medusae, which are structures that look like miniature jellyfish. Each medusa is released into the water and swims away from its parent. Since it has its own tentacles, it can capture food. Some of the medusae are males. They produce sperm cells that carry their DNA blueprints for making more obelia. The rest of the medusae are females, which produce egg cells to carry their DNA blueprints. Both sperm and egg cells are released into the water by the medusae. The sperm are chemically attracted to the eggs. When they find each other, one sperm cell penetrates one egg cell. This is called fertilization. Only when the DNA from the sperm cell joins with the DNA from the egg can the egg cell develop into a new animal.

After it is fertilized, the egg cell divides again and again. As it develops, it swims through the water and is called a planula. Eventually the planula settles on a rock, and a new obelia colony develops from it.

Ferns

Ferns are small plants with upright leaves that grow well in the shade. In most ferns the stem grows underground. When fern leaves first develop, they are tightly rolled up. Then, as each leaf grows, it slowly unwinds.

When ferns reproduce, spores develop on the lower surface of some of the leaves. These spores are released, and some land in moist places where they can grow into green, heart-shaped plants. On one part of the "heart," sperm cells are produced. Close to the notch of the "heart," egg cells form. After it has rained or a heavy dew has settled, the sperm cells swim through the water to reach the egg cells. If fertilization takes place, a new fern plant will grow.

When ferns reproduce, spores are released from the lower surface of some leaves. Spores that land in moist places develop into heart-shaped plants that produce both sperm and egg cells. Sperm cells swim through rainwater or dew to reach the egg cells and fertilize them. Each fertilized egg cell can develop into a new fern plant.

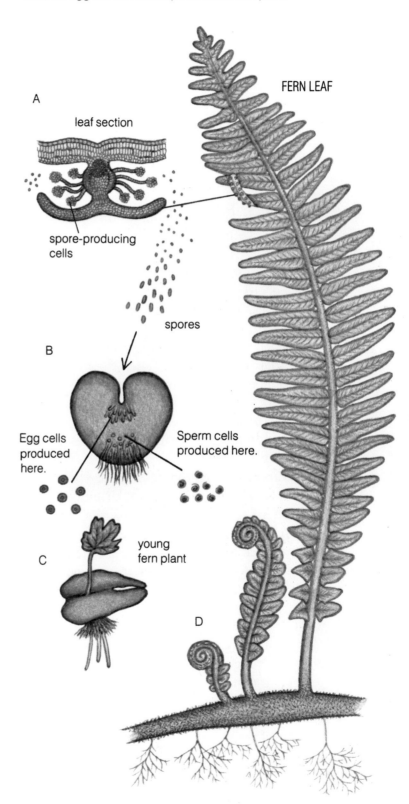

A
leaf section
spore-producing cells
spores
B
Egg cells produced here.
Sperm cells produced here.
young fern plant
C
D
FERN LEAF

73

Trees from Seeds

Pines are large trees that remain green all year long. Their needlelike leaves have thick walls that help prevent water loss, especially in winter. Pine wood is soft, consisting of tracheids (see page 38) but no vessel cells. Like firs, spruces, and cedar trees, pines produce their seeds in cones.

Pine trees produce two kinds of cones. Egg cells form in large female cones. Pollen grains develop in small male cones. Each pollen grain carries DNA molecules from the male to the female cone. Early in the spring millions of pollen grains are released from the male cones and carried for many miles by the wind (step 1).

Female seed cones develop at the tips of new branches. These cones have scales that catch the windblown pollen grains (step 2). At the base of each scale are ovules in which egg cells develop. A sticky substance on the scales helps capture pollen grains. When it dries, it draws a grain into the ovule's opening.

The egg cell and the pollen grain need one year to complete their development. Then the pollen grain grows a pollen tube toward the egg cell. When it reaches the egg cell, the pollen DNA molecules unite with the egg cell DNA molecules (step 3). By the time this fertilization takes place, the cone is green and its scales are tightly closed.

The fertilized egg cell divides and slowly becomes an embryo. An embryo is a plant or animal in the early stages of its life. Surrounding the embryo is stored food. Both the embryo and its food supply become enclosed in a hard, protective seed coat (step 4). This seed takes another year to mature. During this time the cone ripens. When the seeds are released, some fall to the ground but most are carried away by the wind.

All of the activities inside the seed slow down until conditions are right for growing. Then the cells in the embryo that make up the roots absorb water very rapidly. These root cells burst out of the seed coat and grow down in search of water and nutrients (step 5). The rest of the young plant arches until it is standing straight up. It has seed leaves that begin to make food. Below these leaves the tip of the young pine plant begins to grow toward the Sun.

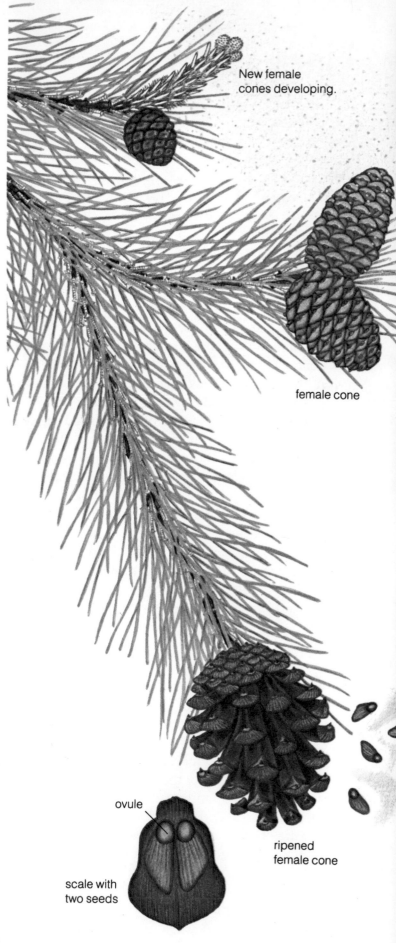

New female cones developing.

female cone

ovule

scale with two seeds

ripened female cone

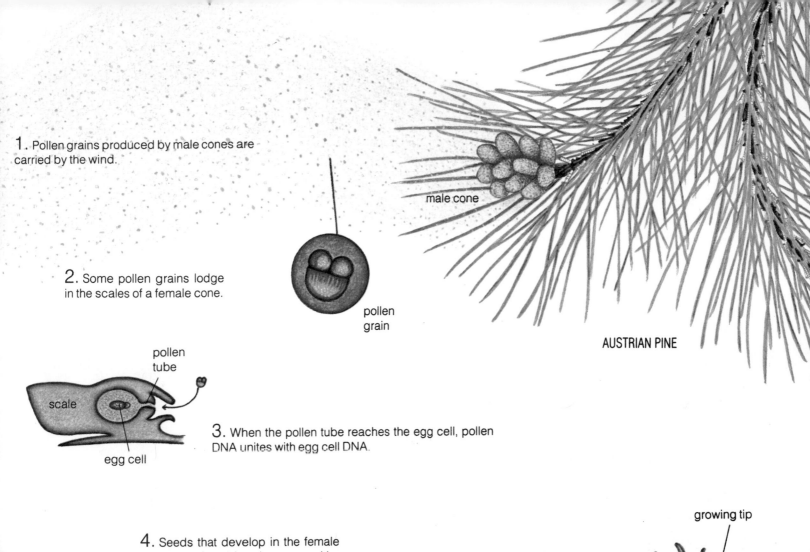

1. Pollen grains produced by male cones are carried by the wind.

male cone

2. Some pollen grains lodge in the scales of a female cone.

pollen grain

AUSTRIAN PINE

pollen tube

scale

egg cell

3. When the pollen tube reaches the egg cell, pollen DNA unites with egg cell DNA.

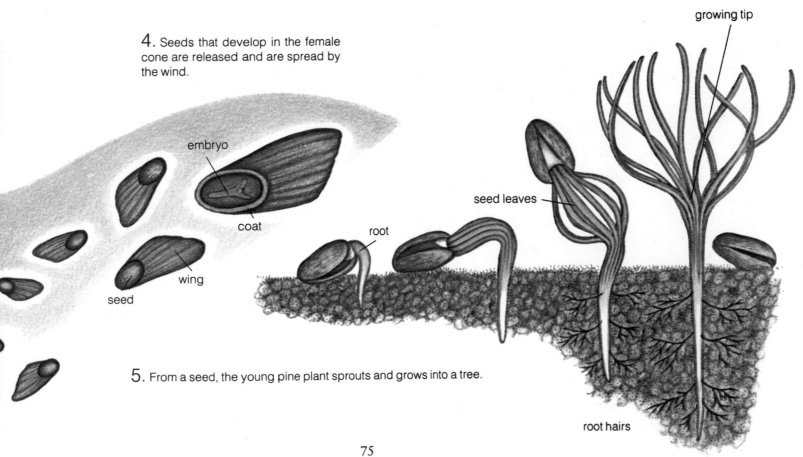

4. Seeds that develop in the female cone are released and are spread by the wind.

growing tip

embryo

coat

seed leaves

root

wing

seed

5. From a seed, the young pine plant sprouts and grows into a tree.

root hairs

The Life of Flowers

Each year millions and millions of flowers blossom all over the world. Flowers have many shapes, sizes, and colors. But no matter what a flower looks like, the job is the same for all flowering plants— flowers take part in reproduction.

Most flowers have four important sets of parts: sepals, petals, stamens, and pistils (carpels). At the base of a flower is a layer of green leaves, called the sepals, which enclose the other flower parts. Above the sepals are the flower petals, which often attract insects. Both petals and sepals protect the inner flower parts.

Attached to the petals are slender stamens. On top of each stamen is a saclike anther in which pollen is produced. The stamen is the male part of a flower.

At the center of many flowers is a pistil, the female portion of a flower. Although flowers can have both male and female parts, some flowers have only male parts and others have only female parts.

Pollen Grains

The male parts of a flower produce pollen grains. Each pollen grain consists of one cell with two nuclei. In these nuclei are the DNA molecules that the pollen grains carry to female flower parts.

Surrounding each pollen grain is an extra-hard cell wall. On the outside of this wall are chemicals that female flower parts have to recognize before the pollen grain can do its job.

Pollination

When pollen grains are fully developed, the wall of the anther bursts open. Since pollen grains can't move by themselves, they have to be carried to the female flower parts. This process is called pollination.

Most plants are pollinated by insects, birds, and the wind. Plants such as grasses give off dry, light pollen grains that are easily picked up and carried by the wind to other flowers. Some plants depend upon insects to carry pollen for them. Insects are attracted to the beautiful colors, patterns, and odors of flowers. They also want to get the sweet-tasting liquid that nectar flowers produce. When insects land on flowers, pollen grains stick to their bodies. Then, when they fly from flower to flower, some of these pollen grains drop and land on female flower parts.

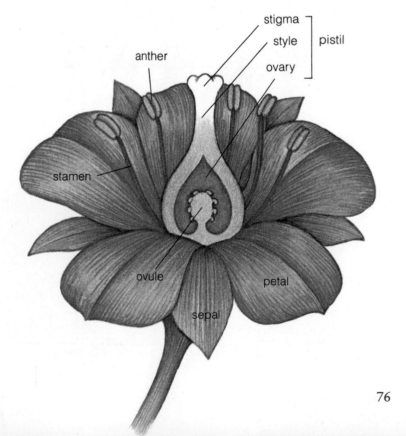

SEEDS FROM FLOWERS A pollen tube grows from a pollen grain that has landed on the stigma of a female flower. This tube delivers two sperm nuclei to an ovule in the ovary. One sperm nucleus fertilizes the egg cell in the ovule. The other helps form a cell that makes food. Every fertilized egg cell can develop into a seed.

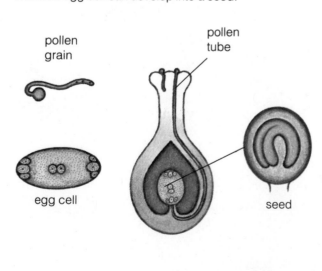

Female Flower Parts

The female portion of a flower has three parts. At the bottom is the ovary, where egg cells are produced. The style rises from the ovary. At the top of the style is a sticky area, the stigma, on which pollen grains have to land.

If pollen grains land on the stigma of the same species of plant, they take in water, swell up, and break open. From each grain, a tiny pollen tube develops, from instructions sent out by one of the nuclei in the pollen grain. This tube digests away the style as it grows toward the ovary. Along the way the other nucleus in the pollen grain divides into two sperm nuclei.

Fertilization

When the pollen tube reaches the bottom of the style, it breaks through into the ovary. The ovary contains ovules, and each ovule holds an egg cell and a group of other cells.

Upon reaching an ovule, the tip of the pollen tube splits open and releases the two sperm nuclei. One sperm nucleus unites with the egg cell, fertilizing it. The second sperm nucleus enters another cell in the ovule to form the endosperm. The endosperm provides food for the embryo as it develops.

The fertilized egg cell divides again and again, forming an embryo. Some of the cells in the embryo will become the root cells of a new plant. Other cells will develop into the stem and leaves.

Seeds and Fruits

As the embryo develops, the walls of the ovary harden into a seed coat that protects the embryo and its food supply. Once the seed has formed, all of the activities of the embryo slow down because the embryo must wait until its seed is carried to a place where it will be able to grow.

Seeds that have winglike parts are scattered by the wind. Those with tiny spines or hooks stick to the skin of animals, are carried from one place to another, and eventually drop to the ground. Some seeds, such as coconuts, float on the water until they wash up on land and split open.

Seeds are also carried away from their plants inside of fruits. After fertilization takes place, the ovary in many flowers ripens into a fruit. Grains, some vegetables, hard-shelled nuts, and the fruits you eat are all ripened ovaries containing seeds. Some fruits fall to the ground, carrying their seeds with them. Others dry out and are blown away by the wind. Some animals, such as squirrels, scatter and bury seeds when they hide nuts. Other animals eat fruits. The seeds inside of an eaten fruit often pass unharmed through an animal's digestive system and are released along with the digestive wastes. A bird can carry a seed for miles before releasing it in wastes.

When conditions are right, seeds germinate (begin to grow). Most seeds need water and the right temperature in order to burst open.

Some flowering plants live for only one growing season. Others live more than one year but stop growing during the winter. At the tips of these plants, hard, protective bud scales form that protect growing cells from drying out. In the spring these buds open and the cells beneath them begin to grow again.

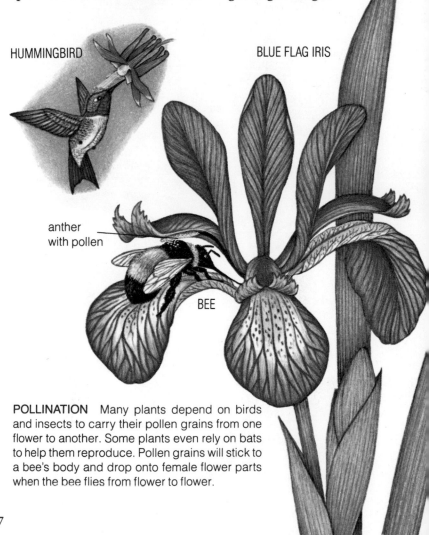

HUMMINGBIRD

BLUE FLAG IRIS

anther with pollen

BEE

POLLINATION Many plants depend on birds and insects to carry their pollen grains from one flower to another. Some plants even rely on bats to help them reproduce. Pollen grains will stick to a bee's body and drop onto female flower parts when the bee flies from flower to flower.

Courtship brings together members of the same species that are ready and willing to mate. This male and female albatross show off markings on their heads and bills that identify their species. Before they will mate, both the male and female have to give each other the right signals in the correct order. These signals include bowing, touching, dancing, and making sounds.

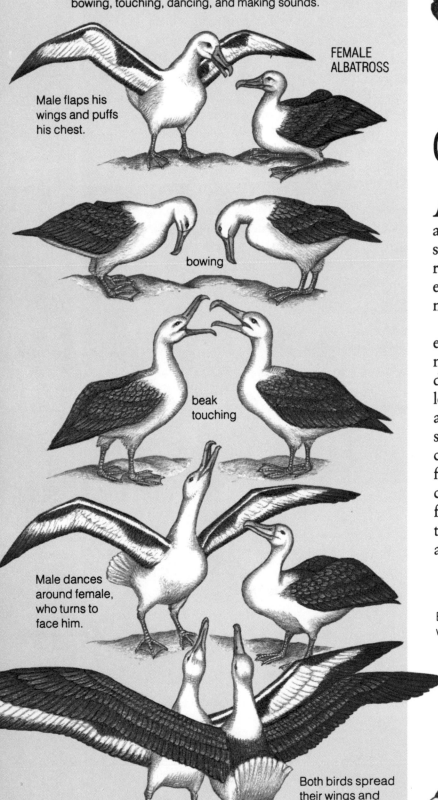

Male flaps his wings and puffs his chest.

FEMALE ALBATROSS

bowing

beak touching

Male dances around female, who turns to face him.

Both birds spread their wings and shriek loudly.

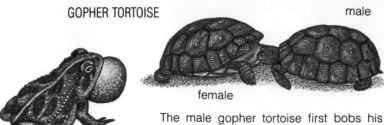

GOPHER TORTOISE

male

female

FOWLER'S TOAD

The male gopher tortoise first bobs his head at the female, then nips at her shell until she agrees to mate. When a male toad croaks, the sounds help a female to find him.

Courtship

All animals have ways of getting males and females together to produce offspring. Since most animals are able to reproduce only during certain seasons of the year, females and males have to be ready to mate at the same time. They also have to let each other know that they are ready and willing to mate. How they do this is called courtship.

In courtship, males and females send signals to each other. One of the most important types of signals is for identification. Since males can only reproduce with females of the same species, they have to let these females know where to find them. Some animals use mating calls or songs to identify themselves. Others give off chemical scents. But identification is only one courtship signal. After two animals find each other, they have to keep on sending the correct signals in the right order. If either the male or female fails to give the correct signal at the proper time, courtship will stop and the animals will move away from each other.

Sticklebacks are small freshwater fish that go

By turning red, a male cuttlefish attracts a female. The fiddler crab waves his big claw in order to attract his mate.

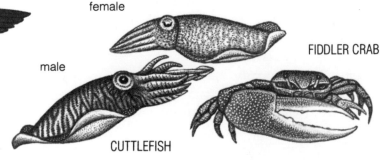

female

male

FIDDLER CRAB

CUTTLEFISH

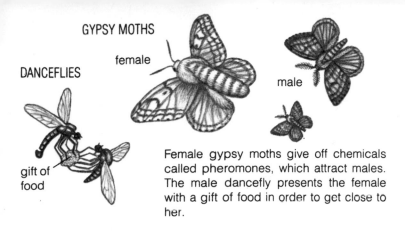

GYPSY MOTHS

female

male

DANCEFLIES

gift of food

Female gypsy moths give off chemicals called pheromones, which attract males. The male dancefly presents the female with a gift of food in order to get close to her.

through many steps when they court. During the spring mating season, male sticklebacks' bellies become bright red. Females are attracted to this bright red coloring. When a male prepares for mating, he chooses a territory, then builds a nest with a tunnel running through the middle of it (see illustration).

Female sticklebacks prepare for mating by producing egg cells. Then they swim near the male's territory. Males are attracted by the females' round bellies, which are swollen with eggs. This swelling signals the male that a female may be ready to mate.

When a female crosses into a male's territory, he swims in a zigzag pattern. If the female raises her head—a signal that she is willing to follow the male—he directs her into the tunnel in his nest. Once she is in the tunnel, the male pokes his nose at her tail, causing her to deposit her eggs in the nest.

As soon as the eggs are laid, the male chases the female away. Then he releases his sperm on top of the eggs. A new stickleback will develop from every egg that is fertilized by a sperm cell.

Other examples of courtship are shown in the illustrations on these pages. In every case, courtship leads to the male releasing his sperm cells in order to fertilize female egg cells.

The male kob prances toward a female who has entered his territory (A). Then he gently touches her thigh to make sure she is willing to mate (B).

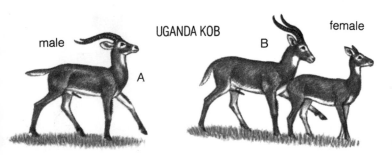

male

UGANDA KOB

female

A

B

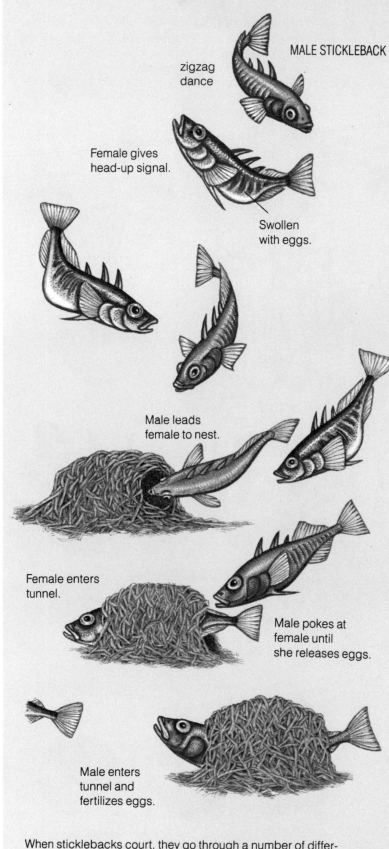

MALE STICKLEBACK

zigzag dance

Female gives head-up signal.

Swollen with eggs.

Male leads female to nest.

Female enters tunnel.

Male pokes at female until she releases eggs.

Male enters tunnel and fertilizes eggs.

When sticklebacks court, they go through a number of different steps that lead to the male releasing sperm cells, which fertilize the female's egg cells.

REPRODUCTION IN HUMANS In males, sperm cells produced in each testis travel through tubes until they are released from the penis. In females, one mature egg cell is released from one of the ovaries about every 28 days. This egg cell is picked up by a fallopian tube and travels toward the vagina. If it is fertilized by a sperm cell, it develops in the uterus for 9 months until birth.

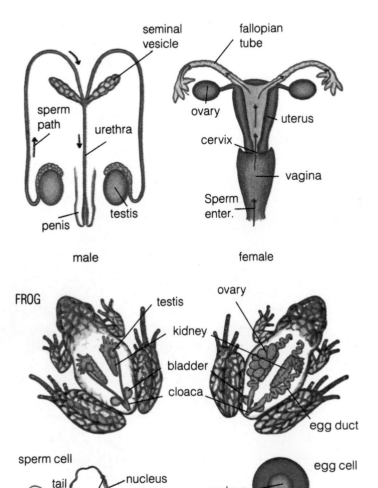

During mating, frogs release sperm cells and egg cells into water.

Filling Earth with Creatures

Animals have special organs for the purpose of reproduction. These organs are different in males and females, because males have to produce sperm cells and females have to develop egg cells.

Sperm Cells

In males, sperm cells are produced in organs called testes. Each testis consists of hundreds of coiled tubes in which millions of sperm cells are produced. Each sperm cell nucleus contains one set of chromosomes. This set is made up of half the total number of chromosomes found in the rest of the cells in the male's body.

Sperm cells look different from other cells. Each sperm cell has very little cytoplasm, and its nucleus is in the head of the sperm. At the very tip of the head is a cap containing enzymes. Sperm cells also have tails, which help them swim toward the egg cell.

Male animals have to reach a certain age before they can make sperm cells. Hormones control the changes in the testes that have to take place to produce sperm.

Egg Cells

Egg cells develop in organs called ovaries. Ovaries contain immature egg cells. When a female animal reaches a certain age, hormones control the changes that cause the egg cells to begin to mature.

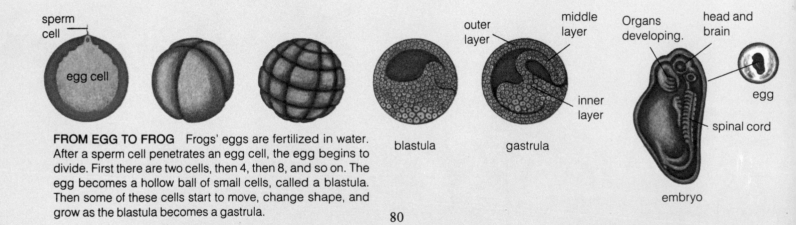

FROM EGG TO FROG Frogs' eggs are fertilized in water. After a sperm cell penetrates an egg cell, the egg begins to divide. First there are two cells, then 4, then 8, and so on. The egg becomes a hollow ball of small cells, called a blastula. Then some of these cells start to move, change shape, and grow as the blastula becomes a gastrula.

Egg cells are much larger than sperm cells. But, like sperm cells, each egg cell contains half the total number of chromosomes found in the rest of the cells in the female's body. Nutrients stored in the cytoplasm of the egg cell are called the yolk.

As egg cells mature they are released by the ovaries and picked up by the egg ducts. In humans, one mature egg cell is given off about every 28 days. In most animals, mature egg cells are released only during the mating season.

Mating

Courtship brings together males and females of the same species when both are ready to mate. At mating, males have to release their sperm cells from their bodies. Sperm travel through tubes to an opening from which they are given off. In many kinds of animals, sperm are released from an organ called the penis.

In most fish and amphibians, females release their eggs outside of their bodies when they mate. Males then cover these eggs with their sperm. A different sperm cell has to penetrate each egg cell to fertilize it. Eggs and sperm that don't unite die.

In reptiles, birds, land animals, and some fish and amphibians, eggs are fertilized while they are inside of the female's body. In some animals, sperm are given off into the female's cloaca (page 43); in other kinds of animals, they are released into the vagina, a cavity leading to the egg ducts. Once released, the sperm swim toward the egg cells. Although many sperm never reach the egg cell, it only takes one sperm cell out of the millions released to fertilize one egg cell.

Fertilization

When a sperm cell reaches an egg cell, the tip of the sperm gives off its enzymes. These help the head of the sperm cell penetrate the egg cell membrane. Once this occurs, the sperm nucleus, carrying the male DNA molecules, moves through the egg until its chromosomes unite with those in the egg cell. This fertilizes the egg, making it capable of forming a new animal. As soon as the egg is penetrated, its outer membrane changes, making it impossible for any other sperm cells to enter the egg.

Development

After the egg cell is fertilized, it begins to divide. The first division forms two cells. These two cells divide and make four cells. This process continues, but none of the cells grow yet. As each division takes place, the cells become smaller and smaller. In many animals, all of these small cells form a hollow ball, called a blastula, which is only one cell thick and no bigger than the original egg cell. At this early stage of development the egg is already an embryo.

The embryo remains a hollow ball of cells until a group of cells move inward, forming a second layer of cells. This part of development is called gastrulation. During gastrulation, cells move, change shape, divide, and redivide. A third layer of cells develops between the first two, and parts of the embryo fold while other parts grow in size.

As the cell layers develop, they use up the energy stored in the egg yolk. Cells in the outer layer slowly develop into skin cells and into the cells that make up the nervous system. Cells in the middle layer become muscle, bone, and blood cells. Parts of the

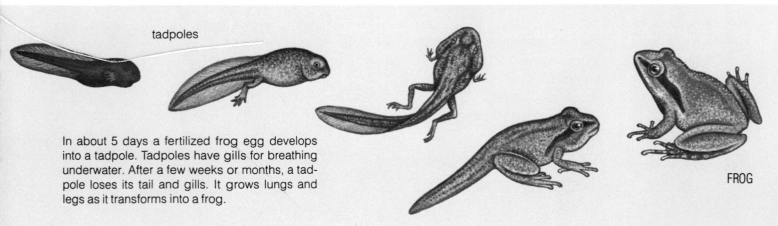

tadpoles

In about 5 days a fertilized frog egg develops into a tadpole. Tadpoles have gills for breathing underwater. After a few weeks or months, a tadpole loses its tail and gills. It grows lungs and legs as it transforms into a frog.

FROG

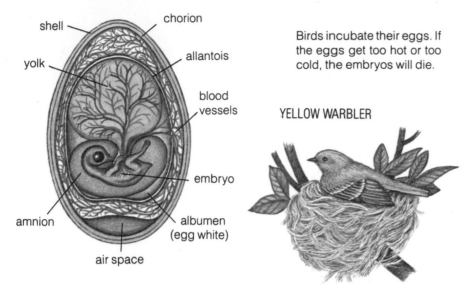

shell · chorion · yolk · allantois · blood vessels · embryo · amnion · albumen (egg white) · air space

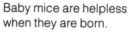

YELLOW WARBLER

Birds incubate their eggs. If the eggs get too hot or too cold, the embryos will die.

INSIDE THE EGG In its egg, a chick embryo is surrounded by four membranes. Blood vessels in the yolk sac membrane carry food from the yolk to the embryo. The amnion contains a protective fluid, and the allantois collects wastes. Lining the shell is the moist chorion, used for gas exchange.

Whales are mammals that feed mother's milk to their young.

Baby mice are helpless when they are born.

digestive system and respiratory system develop from cells in the inner layer of the embryo.

It takes different lengths of time for different animals to develop. By the time each animal is born, its tissues and organs have formed according to the instructions contained in the DNA molecules it received from its parents.

Tadpoles and Frogs

Frog eggs are fertilized in the water. One female frog can give off hundreds of eggs at the same time. All are covered in a jellylike substance that hardens after fertilization. Even with this protection, many eggs die when they are damaged or eaten by other animals.

A fertilized frog egg develops into a tadpole in about five days. Tadpoles can swim and find food for themselves. They have gills for breathing underwater.

As it grows, a tadpole undergoes metamorphosis and becomes a frog. Its tail shrinks, it grows legs, and its muscles and bones develop. The gills disappear and lungs form. The frog, now able to breathe air, can leave the water and live on land.

Eggs and Chickens

In chickens and other birds, an egg cell is fertilized inside the female's body and immediately begins to develop. As it does, it is surrounded by a protein called albumen (egg white), then covered in a hard shell that is formed from glands in the egg duct. Within about half a day the bird lays the egg. Hens lay their eggs even if they have not been fertilized. These unfertilized eggs that you eat are really very large single cells surrounded by albumen and a shell.

Hens sit on their fertilized eggs for 21 days, keeping them at the temperature required by the embryo to develop. The egg contains all the food the embryo needs to grow. Oxygen passes in through pores in the shell, and carbon dioxide is given off the same way.

After 21 days the baby bird pecks at the shell until it breaks. Within hours of hatching, baby chicks can run and get their own food. Other species of birds are born helpless. They need to be protected and fed by their parents until they learn to fly and can find food for themselves.

Reptiles

Like birds, most female reptiles lay their eggs after the eggs have been fertilized inside their body. But before these eggs are laid, they are covered in a tough, leathery shell. Reptiles often bury their eggs so other animals won't find them and eat them.

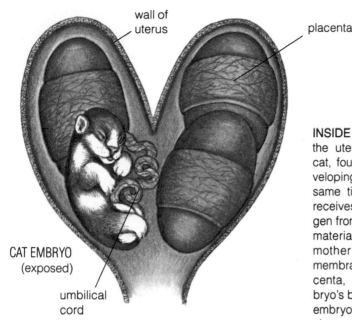

wall of uterus

placenta

CAT EMBRYO (exposed)

umbilical cord

INSIDE THE UTERUS In the uterus of this female cat, four embryos are developing into babies at the same time. Each embryo receives nutrients and oxygen from its mother. These materials move from the mother's blood, through membranes called the placenta, and into the embryo's blood vessels. Each embryo is attached to its placenta by the umbilical cord.

Although the platypus lays eggs, she also feeds her babies milk.

DUCK-BILLED PLATYPUS

actual size at birth

KANGAROO

When a baby kangaroo is born, it is hardly developed. It completes its development inside of its mother's pouch, where it is fed her milk.

Some reptiles, such as alligators, care for their young after they hatch from their eggs. Most other reptile babies, though, are on their own from the moment they hatch.

Mammals

Many female land animals carry their embryos inside their bodies until the embryos have developed enough to be born. In these animals, fertilized egg cells move down the egg ducts until they reach the uterus (page 80), where they start to divide.

Eggs that develop in the uterus have very little stored food, so they have to get their nutrients from their mother. These eggs attach to the wall of the uterus, where membranes called a placenta form. Each embryo is connected to the placenta by the umbilical cord. The embryo's blood vessels run through this cord. Nutrients and oxygen cross from the mother's bloodstream, through the membranes of the placenta, and into the blood vessels of the embryo. Wastes produced by the embryo travel in the opposite direction and are eliminated by the mother. During development, embryos are surrounded by a fluid that absorbs shocks.

Mice develop, or gestate, in the uterus for 20 days before they are ready to be born. Cats gestate for 9 weeks, and elephants need 20 months. It takes humans 9 months to develop. At birth, animals have to be developed enough to be able to breathe for themselves. Their hearts have to pump blood to all parts of their bodies and they have to be able to get rid of their own wastes. Some animals, such as deer and horses, are so developed that they can move around very soon after they are born.

Animals that feed milk to their newborn are called mammals. The mother's milk is given off by the mammary glands (page 48). The milk contains vitamins, minerals, and proteins. It also contains antibodies from the mother that protect the newborn from disease until the immune system takes over. Mammals take care of their young until they are able to take care of themselves. Kangaroos, koala bears, and opossums are mammals whose embryos stay in the uterus for only a short time. Their young are born hardly developed and have to crawl into their mother's pouch, where they drink milk until they complete their development. Newborn human babies are quite helpless and need a lot of care from their parents. After birth all animals grow and continue to develop into adults. They reach a time when they, too, can become parents. In this way, life is passed on from one generation to the next.

At Life's Edge

BACTERIAL VIRUS

DNA

head

tail

tail fiber

A
virus

B
DNA from virus

C
DNA replicates.

New virus particles form.

D

New viruses released from cell.

E
virus DNA

bacterial DNA

VIRUSES When this virus lands on a bacterial cell (A), it injects its DNA inside the cell (B). The viral DNA takes over the cell's activities and makes more virus parts (C). These parts assemble into about 100 new viruses, which cause the cell to burst (D). Sometimes viral DNA does not make new viruses. Instead, it joins up with the DNA in the cell (E) and is carried along until it is ready to reproduce. Many diseases, such as smallpox, pneumonia, influenza, and rabies, are caused by viruses. Herpes viruses (right) infect animal cells, and tobacco mosaic viruses infect plant cells.

Viruses are tiny particles that are different from every living cell. They have no organelles, they can't make their own proteins, and they can't produce ATP molecules for energy. Viruses don't take in food and don't carry on respiration. About the only thing that viruses do that living cells do is reproduce. But viruses can't even reproduce by themselves. They have to take over living cells and reproduce inside of them. Some viruses take over animal cells, some take over plant cells, and some take over bacteria.

Many viruses consist of a DNA molecule surrounded by a protective protein covering, called the head. A few kinds of viruses contain an RNA molecule (page 23) instead of a DNA molecule. Attached to the head of a virus is often a hollow cylinder, called the tail, which is made of proteins. At the end of the tail are long, thin fibers.

Using its tail fibers, a virus can attach itself to a living cell. Once attached, the hollow tail contracts, injecting the viral DNA into the cell. Inside the cell, the viral DNA can take over the cell's activities. Viral genes send out their own messenger RNA instructions for making new virus parts. These messenger RNA molecules use the cell's ribosomes to make these virus parts. Many copies of the virus DNA molecule are made. Then the parts assemble into new virus particles. When the particles are complete, they can cause the cell to burst open and release them.

Sometimes viruses don't immediately take over the cells they infect. Instead, the virus DNA molecule joins up with a DNA molecule in the cell. If the cell divides, each daughter cell gets a copy of the virus DNA. At a certain time, when conditions are right, the virus DNA molecule frees itself, takes over the cell, and makes new virus particles.

RNA

proteins

HERPES VIRUS

TOBACCO MOSAIC VIRUS

The Science of Life

All of the information in this book was collected by men and women studying life on Earth. This information and much more makes up biology, the science of life.

Biologists observe living things. They ask questions about how living cells work. Scientists search for answers to their questions by doing experiments—special procedures that are set up to answer a question. Performing experiments requires special tools, such as microscopes. Light microscopes allow scientists to look at plant and animal cells. With an electron microscope, a tiny virus can be photographed.

Sometimes experiments work; sometimes they don't. Every experiment has to be done at least twice to make certain that it can be repeated. When an experiment works, new facts are added to what is already known about life on Earth. New facts lead to more questions and more experiments.

Facts and Theories

Biologists often try to explain how things work before they have done their experiments. Their explanations are called theories. Theories have to be tested by doing the right experiments. If a scientist proves that a theory is correct, the theory becomes a fact.

One of the most famous theories is the theory of evolution. This theory tries to explain how life on Earth came about. According to this theory, life developed on Earth billions of years ago. At first there were only simple living cells that multiplied. Sometimes slight changes occurred in the DNA of some of these simple creatures. Changes in the DNA molecules caused proteins and other cell parts to change. Such changes made some creatures slightly different from the rest. These changes in the DNA molecules were passed on from one generation to the next.

Each kind of creature had to compete with all the rest for food, water, oxygen, minerals, and other materials. Some creatures were more successful than others at getting the things they needed, because of the ways in which they were different. Others were not as fit for survival and died off.

As time passed, more and more creatures changed. Very, very slowly the changes began to add up. Over many generations new creatures developed as one type of living thing slowly changed into another. The changes never stopped happening. Like branches continually growing on a tree, every type of living thing found on Earth today gradually developed from the first simple creatures.

No one has been able to prove that this is the way life on Earth developed. Even so, most scientists believe that the theory of evolution is true. It will continue to be called a theory until someone performs experiments to prove it.

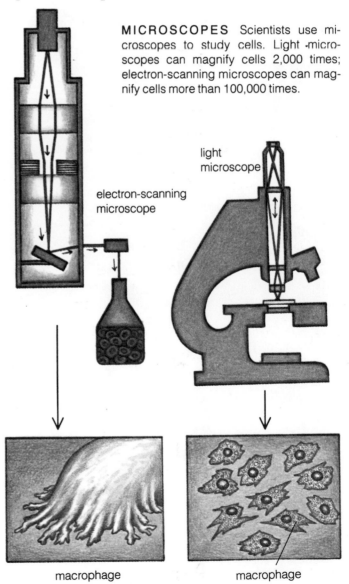

MICROSCOPES Scientists use microscopes to study cells. Light microscopes can magnify cells 2,000 times; electron-scanning microscopes can magnify cells more than 100,000 times.

light microscope

electron-scanning microscope

macrophage

macrophage

PTERODON

30-inch DRAGONFLY

DUCK-BILLED DINOSAUR

GIANT HORSETAIL

8-inch COCKROACH

NAUTILOID

GIANT FERN

TRILOBITE

STELLER'S SEA COW

GREAT AUK

DODO

SABER-TOOTHED CAT

EXTINCTION Scientists believe that floods, droughts, diseases, and climate changes have caused many species to die out completely. Other species have been hunted down until there were none left. Even if you spent your life searching for these plants and animals, you would not find them. They are gone forever.

Into the Future

This is a very exciting time for the science of biology. Every day new facts are being learned about DNA, proteins, membranes, viruses, and cells. Using special enzymes, scientists are now able to remove DNA molecules from cells and cut them into pieces. They can then experiment with the pieces by putting them into different cells. By gene splicing, they can also join the pieces to other DNA molecules.

Scientists have learned how to take cells out of plants, animals, and human beings and grow these cells in test tubes. By doing experiments with cells and molecules like DNA, scientists hope to cure diseases, produce vaccines that will prevent other diseases, and figure out how to grow enough food to feed all of the people living on Earth. During your lifetime many of these great discoveries will be made. And some of you will be making them.

Life on Earth

Most organisms produce as many offspring as they can. Very few offspring survive because most are eaten. Some also lose their lives because of diseases, floods, droughts, and earthquakes. And many other plants and animals have died because of some of the ways human beings live.

The wonders of science have placed great power in the hands of men and women. With this power people take living space away from other organisms and use it for houses, factories, and roadways. As human populations expand they use up resources, such as trees, minerals, oil, and gas. Food is needed for more and more people. Industries and cars produce chemical and radioactive wastes, which are released into the air, water, and soil. When these wastes are taken into the bodies of living things, tissues and organs can be damaged, sometimes so badly that creatures are killed. Many chemicals are stored in plant and animal bodies. When people eat these plants and animals or drink dirty water or breathe polluted air, they are harmed too.

In spite of all of these ways in which animals and plants can lose their lives, enough of most species survive to produce more offspring. But the numbers of some kinds of animals and plants have become very low. If the members of these species continue to die off, there will be so few left that they won't be able to find each other to reproduce. Then the entire species will become extinct and be lost forever.

At the Controls

There are many things we can do to stop the needless loss of life on Earth. We can rescue animals and plants when floods and other natural disasters put them in danger. To make up for the lands we have cleared for ourselves, we can set aside parks and preserves where plants and animals can live and reproduce. We can pass laws that will protect endangered species. Scientific knowledge can be used to clean up our chemical wastes, make our air and water fresh again, and restore our soil. As we use up trees, we can plant new ones to take their place. We can also learn to be more careful about how we use our precious resources. And we can continue to study all forms of life because it is from them that we can learn about our living world.

Along with all other organisms, we are members of the family of living things and Earth is our home. It has to be cared for and protected or nothing will be able to live on it.

Life on Earth depends upon the relationships between living things and the world around them. Plants and animals provide food, oxygen, and energy. Bacteria and fungi recycle elements such as carbon and nitrogen. Organisms rely on Earth for water, air, minerals, soil, and shelter.

The efforts we make for the survival of every different kind of living thing are vitally important. After all, in the entire Universe there is nothing quite like life on Earth.

SPECIES IN DANGER The numbers of all these animals have dropped so low that they are in danger of becoming extinct. Even the blue whale, the largest creature on Earth, is in danger. Along with many others, these animals have to be protected so that they can reproduce and build up their numbers.

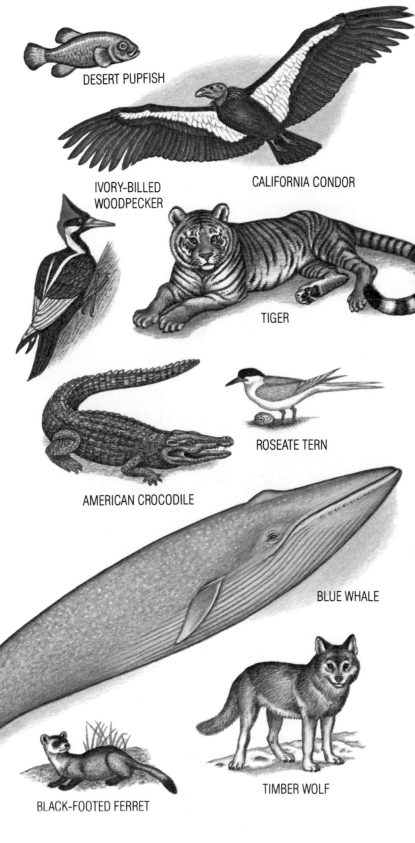

DESERT PUPFISH

IVORY-BILLED WOODPECKER

CALIFORNIA CONDOR

TIGER

AMERICAN CROCODILE

ROSEATE TERN

BLUE WHALE

GREEN TURTLE

BLACK-FOOTED FERRET

TIMBER WOLF

The Family of Living Things

Many scientists divide all living things into five main groups, called kingdoms. Three of these kingdoms—monera, protist, and animal—are shown here. They include single-celled organisms and animals without backbones, or invertebrates. Most animals living on Earth are invertebrates.

Each kingdom is divided into smaller groups. All of the members of a group have things in common with each other. In most cases, only one kind of organism is shown from each group.

Some groups are divided even further. Arthropods, for example, are divided into insects, crabs, spiders, centipedes, and other groups. There are about one million species of insects. The ladybug shown here stands for all these insects. The rest of the groups that make up the animal kingdom are shown on the next two pages.

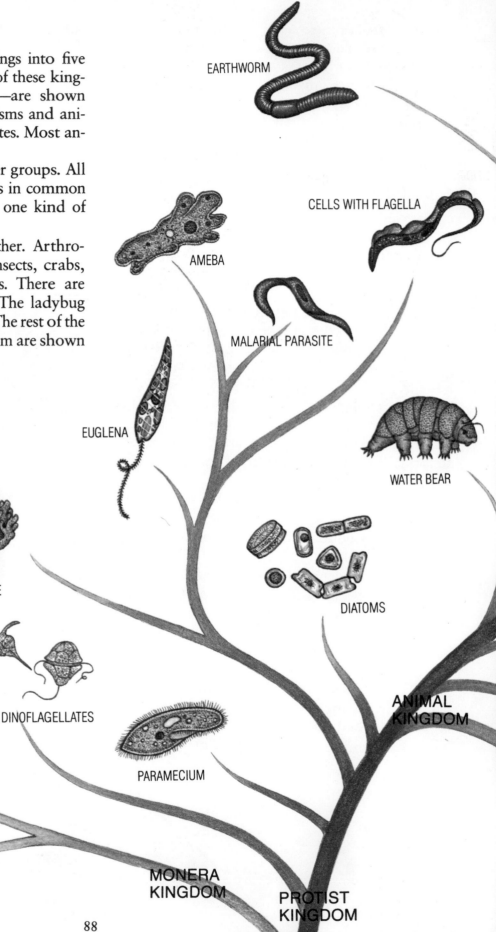

EARTHWORM

CELLS WITH FLAGELLA

AMEBA

MALARIAL PARASITE

EUGLENA

WATER BEAR

DIATOMS

SPONGE

DINOFLAGELLATES

BLUE-GREEN ALGAE

PARAMECIUM

BACTERIA

ANIMAL KINGDOM

MONERA KINGDOM

PROTIST KINGDOM

88

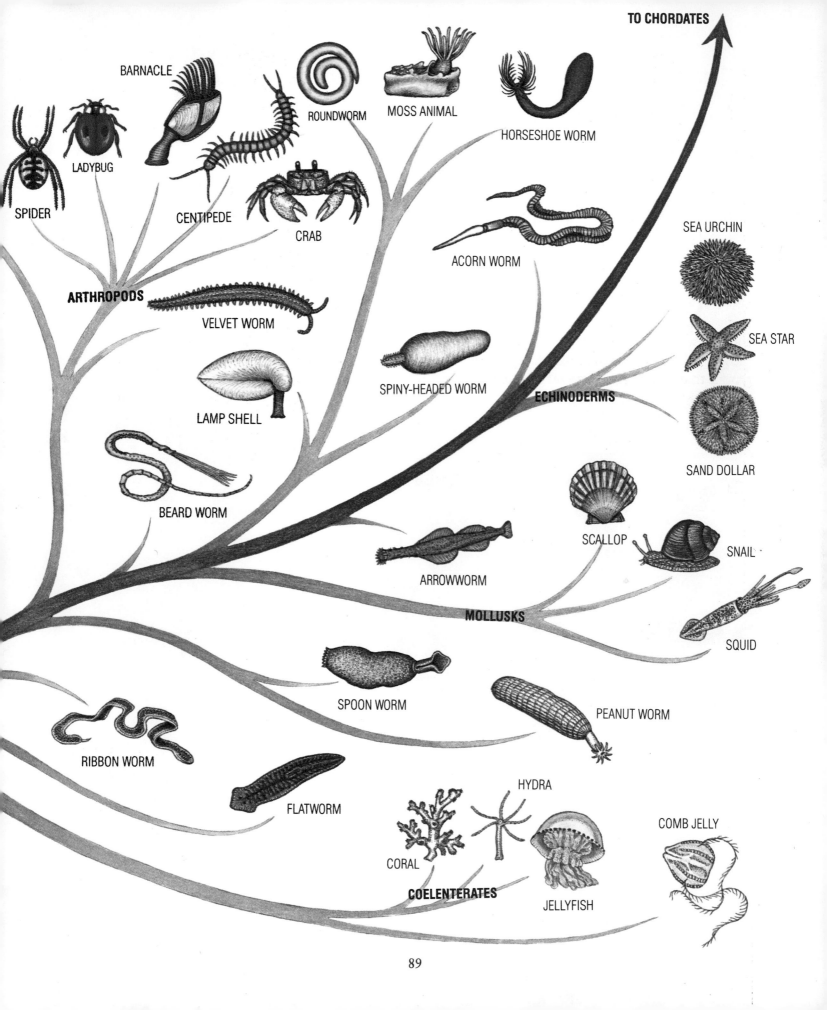

TO CHORDATES

BARNACLE

ROUNDWORM

MOSS ANIMAL

LADYBUG

HORSESHOE WORM

SPIDER

CENTIPEDE

CRAB

SEA URCHIN

ACORN WORM

ARTHROPODS

VELVET WORM

SEA STAR

SPINY-HEADED WORM

LAMP SHELL

ECHINODERMS

SAND DOLLAR

BEARD WORM

SCALLOP

SNAIL

ARROWWORM

MOLLUSKS

SQUID

SPOON WORM

PEANUT WORM

RIBBON WORM

HYDRA

FLATWORM

COMB JELLY

CORAL

COELENTERATES

JELLYFISH

89

The Family of Living Things

The animals shown on these two pages are the ones you probably know best. All of them belong to the same main group, called chordates. Chordates are divided into many smaller groups, most of which contain animals with backbones (vertebrates). There are more than 35,000 different species of vertebrates. Scientists place human beings in the same group as gorillas and other primates.

CAMEL

AARDVARK

HORSE

HYRAX

ELEPHANT

MANATEE

SEAHORSE

MOORISH IDOL

PERCH

EEL

CATFISH

BONY FISHES

BOWFIN

GAR

SHARK

STURGEON

RAY

CHIMERA

LAMPREY

LUNGFISH

COELACANTH

HAGFISH

FISHES

ANIMAL KINGDOM
(continued)   90

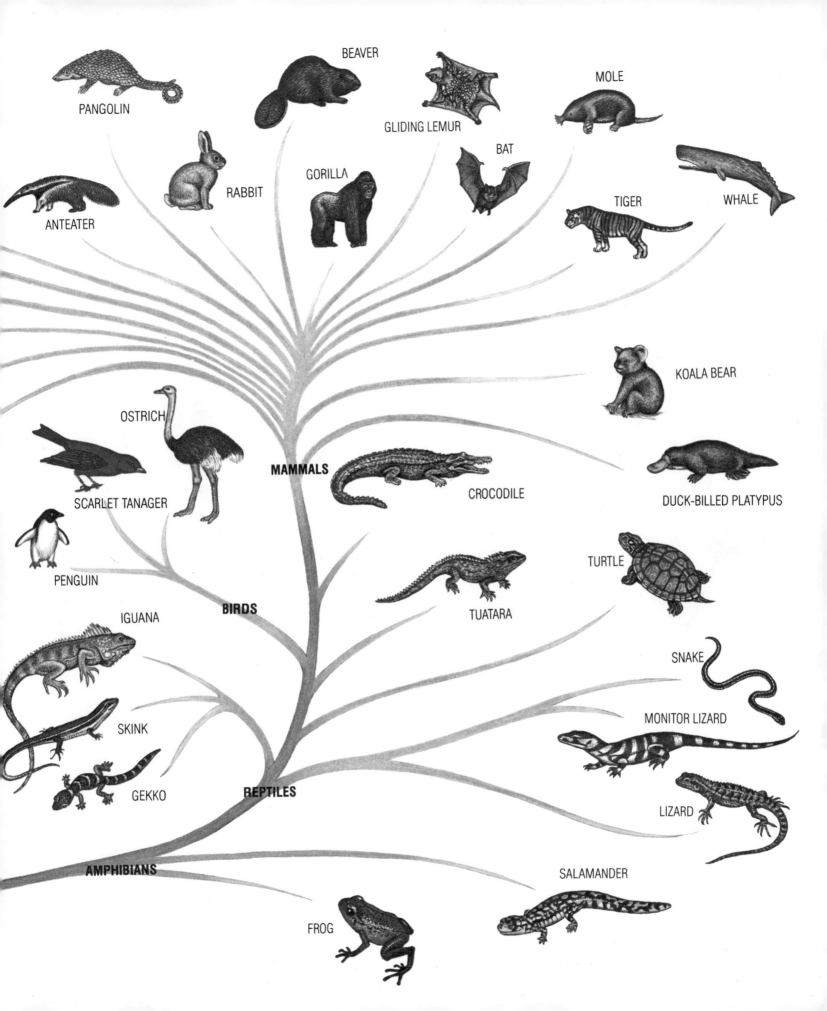

PANGOLIN

BEAVER

GLIDING LEMUR

MOLE

ANTEATER

RABBIT

GORILLA

BAT

TIGER

WHALE

KOALA BEAR

OSTRICH

MAMMALS

CROCODILE

DUCK-BILLED PLATYPUS

SCARLET TANAGER

PENGUIN

BIRDS

TURTLE

TUATARA

SNAKE

IGUANA

MONITOR LIZARD

SKINK

REPTILES

LIZARD

GEKKO

AMPHIBIANS

SALAMANDER

FROG

The Family of Living Things

These two pages present the fungus kingdom and the plant kingdom. There are more than 200,000 species of fungi and more than 250,000 species of plants.

You are probably familiar with many of the plants shown here. But just as on the previous pages, each picture represents only one plant in the entire group. For example, the rose group contains more than 2,000 different kinds of related plants. Besides roses, this group includes apple trees, almond trees, cherry trees, peach trees, and blackberry bushes.

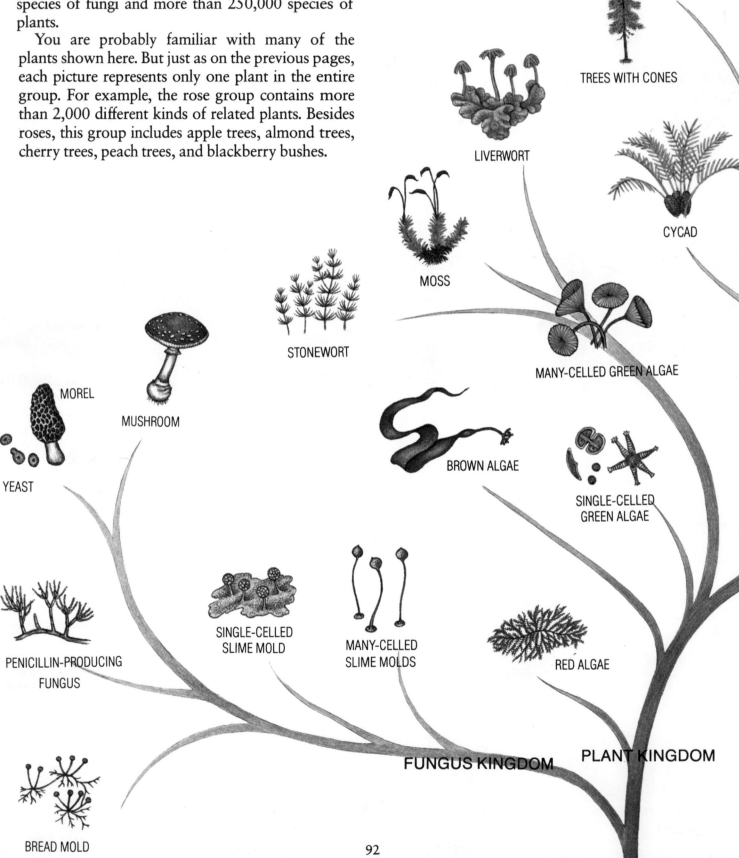

TREES WITH CONES

LIVERWORT

CYCAD

MOSS

STONEWORT

MANY-CELLED GREEN ALGAE

MOREL

MUSHROOM

BROWN ALGAE

SINGLE-CELLED
GREEN ALGAE

YEAST

PENICILLIN-PRODUCING
FUNGUS

SINGLE-CELLED
SLIME MOLD

MANY-CELLED
SLIME MOLDS

RED ALGAE

FUNGUS KINGDOM

PLANT KINGDOM

BREAD MOLD

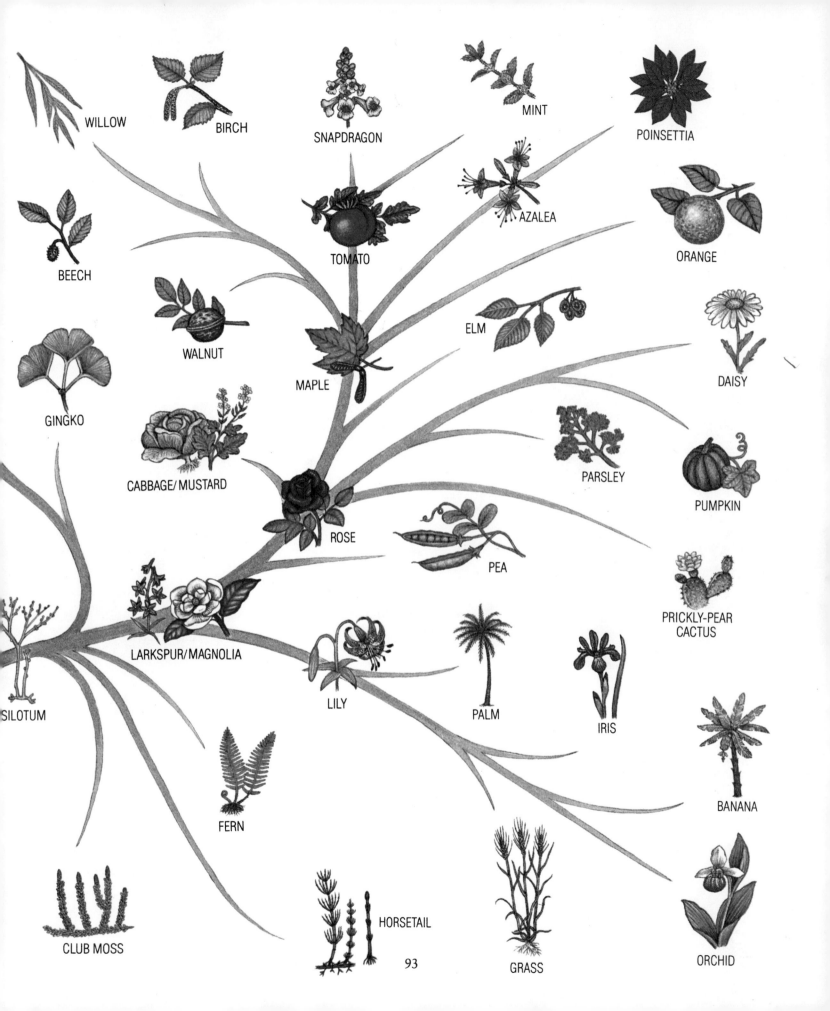

WILLOW

BIRCH

SNAPDRAGON

MINT

POINSETTIA

AZALEA

BEECH

TOMATO

ORANGE

WALNUT

ELM

DAISY

GINGKO

CABBAGE/ MUSTARD

MAPLE

PARSLEY

PUMPKIN

ROSE

PEA

PRICKLY-PEAR
CACTUS

SILOTUM

LARKSPUR/ MAGNOLIA

LILY

PALM

IRIS

BANANA

FERN

CLUB MOSS

HORSETAIL

93

GRASS

ORCHID

INDEX

Page numbers in *italic type* refer to material in illustrations and captions.